3 ⁰⁰
189p
1970

HELPING
EACH OTHER
BE HUMAN

HELPING
EACH OTHER
BE HUMAN

R. Lofton Hudson

WORD BOOKS, *Publisher*

Waco, Texas   London, England

Grateful acknowledgment is made for the use of copyright material as
follows:

Quotations from the Revised Standard Version of the Bible, copyright 1946
and 1952 by the Division of Christian Education of the National Council of
Churches of Christ in the United States of America. Used by permission.

Quotations from *The New Testament in the Language of the People,* by
Charles B. Williams, copyright 1955. Used by permission of Moody Press,
Moody Bible Institute of Chicago.

Quotations from *The New English Bible New Testament* © The Delegates
of The Oxford University Press and The Syndics of the Cambridge University Press 1961. Reprinted by permission.

Quotations from *The New Testament, An American Translation,* by Edgar
Goodspeed.

Quotations from the Today's English Version of the New Testament. Copyright © American Bible Society 1966.

Quotation from *The New Testament in Modern English* by J. B. Phillips.
© J. B. Phillips 1958. Used by permission of The Macmillan Company.

Library of Congress catalog card number: 79-85831

Printed in the United States of America.

ACKNOWLEDGMENTS

The author wishes to express his gratitude to the following individuals and publishers who made possible the inclusion of previously published materials in this book:

Basic Books Inc., for a quotation from *Neurotic Interaction in Marriage,* edited by Victor W. Eisenstein, M.D., copyright © 1956.

Damila Music Co., Inc., for a quotation from the song "I've Gotta Be Me."

For the translation of a poem of Laotzu, copyright © 1944 by Witter Bynner, reprinted from *The Way of Life According to Laotzu,* translated by Witter Bynner, by permission of The John Day Company, Inc., publisher.

For the poem "Simply Assisting God" from *Grooks* 1 by Piet Hein; © 1966; Doubleday & Co., N. Y., edition 1969. By permission of the author.

Harper & Row, Publishers, Incorporated, for quotations from *Reality Therapy* by William Glasser, M.D., copyright 1965.

Alfred A. Knopf, Inc., for a quotation from *The Plague* by Albert Camus, copyright 1948; and for a quotation from "The Night of Truth" in *Resistance, Rebellion, and Death, by* Albert Camus, copyright 1960.

For the poem "Outwitted" by Edwin Markham, reprinted by permission of Virgil Markham.

William Morrow & Company, Inc., for a quotation from *Man's Right To Be Human* by George Christian Anderson, copyright © 1959 by George Christian Anderson.

George Allen Unwin Ltd., for a quotation from *The Knowledge of Man* by Martin Buber, © 1965, Martin Buber and Maurice Friedman.

Westminster Press for quotations from *Living Without God Before God* by David O. Woodyard, copyright © 1968, The Westminster Press.

For the poem "Courage" from *Burning Bush* by Karle Wilson Baker. Copyright © 1922 by Yale University Press.

CONTENTS

CHAPTER ONE

Helping Each Other
Be Human

I have had a feeling for years that Christianity drives off a lot of sound, basically good people because it is misunderstood. And precisely at the point of how it sees us as human beings. The way the Christian message is preached, and especially the way it is taught in Sunday school and in instruction classes, man gets blacklisted and finds it hard to hold his indoctrinated head up.

In our talk of the depravity of man, his lostness, original sin, and natural perversity we have contributed to knocking man right out of his tree, at least those who take it seriously. He seems to read it that religion is saying that he is all bad, a sinner spelled with a capital S, a rat fink, a louse, as well as a square and a bourgeois. In the prayer books you read such devastating clauses as we confess "our manifold sins and wickedness" and "there is no health in us," us "miserable sinners." This kind of "imprinting" probably does a great deal of harm and hardly brings anyone to renewal.

At this point I can see red flags running up and individuals from various religious persuasions asking: "Do you or don't you believe in original sin?" "Do you deny the doctrine of the depravity of man?" "Don't you believe that all have sinned and come short of the glory of God?"

I even believe that they have come short of the glory of man. Furthermore, I don't think that "original sin" explains anything — aside from the fact that sin is usually not very orig-

9

inal. If we mean that man is who he is, at times brutish, lousy, egocentric, narcissistic, and perverse, I will agree. If we mean that all men tend to self-destruct and fall short of what they might become, are but caricatures of what might have been, I will buy that. If we mean by "total depravity" that man is totally bad, which theologians rarely mean, I will not buy that. It is a fact, however, that everything man touches turns to lead, not gold, that we are extremely limited, finite, and that we do not make much progress as human beings. We are certainly, as someone has said, "the unfinished animal."

But until recently, and in many groups yet, one senses that when they talk or sing about religion they express a genuine contempt for man. He, at best, is a sheep. Their God-talk, in addition to such maligning words as I have mentioned above, often speaks of "unbelievers" and "sinners" and "pagans" (formerly "heathen"), as the Pharisees did of tax collectors and sinners, as if they are a different kind of people, spiritual pariahs, whose duty is and deserves to be extinction or eternal torture. In a world where we so easily become "ittified" (an "it" instead of a person) or "thingified," where we are depersonalized, and are even referred to by numbers instead of names, Christianity should do everything it can to help individuals feel valued, respected, and appreciated.

One of my friends, a trained pastoral counselor, appeared before a committee of the Internal Revenue Service to interpret to them what a certified pastoral counselor does. Among other things he attempted to show that for this type of therapy there was always an emphasis on what it meant to be a person. He contended that even among professionals it is easy for the individual to be treated like a machine which is to be oiled or repaired, factory line fashion, rather than have someone take the time to understand his fears, his lack of meaning, and his frustrated hopes as a human being. One of the IRS men argued that he did not believe any depersonalizing was the cause of emotional illness problems. Reference was made by the counselor to an article on the subject. When the IRS man expressed eagerness to see it, the counselor asked him to put his name and address on a piece of paper and he would be glad to drop it in the mail. To the counselor's amazement, the man did not use his name at all, but a number! It wasn't 007 but one that apparently catered to a machine mail distributor.

We have two problems before us, then. First, there is the guilt-ridden, self-effacing, worm of the dust, tendency that runs very deep in our culture. Second, the alienation, anonymity, impersonalizing aspects of our living which turns us from being either homo sapiens or homo ludens (happiness) in becoming organization men and button punching men who might well be listed homo mechanicus or homo consumens.

Is Man Still Lost?

To be more precise, the Church in the past has worked at getting men's souls saved. Now they really have that task cut out for them. Man may not use the same words. He doesn't feel "condemned and unclean" even though the hymnology still contains some of this verbiage. He does feel that he is losing his "self." Further, that this self cannot be reclaimed except in relationships. If something is not done in a hurry — the herd instinct notwithstanding — he will die of coldness, distance, and estrangement.

Where, then, can the Church lay ahold of the problem of how to think of man? Shall we go back to Freud's dark picture of man laden with his Oedipus complexes, eaten up by his cancerous narcissism, and foredoomed by his death instinct? Hardly. Shall we subscribe to the naive optimism of the Renaissance and the Enlightenment and declare that all evil in man is merely the result of his circumstances, that he is basically good and perfectible, that we need merely to change his circumstances (as attempted in Communism) and his native goodness will come through? Such a dream or hope is almost

inspiring. The facts which contradict it, however, keep stab-
bing us awake and reminding us to put on our glasses.

Perhaps we would be better off if we adopt a meta-theolog-
ical (alongside theology) and meta-psychological and even
meta-philosophical approach and begin with man as he is. He
often looks like a piece of human capital badly invested. But
alongside these sorry actions we see heroism, honesty, sacrifice
for convictions' sake, willingness to give of self, and intelligent
attempts to care for one's neighbor at least as much as self.

As one of my friends who has lived many years said to me,
"The thing that amazes me about human beings is the goodness
of some pretty bad people I have known, and on the other
hand the surprising badness of some otherwise good people; if
they would be one way or the other, I could find some way to
work with them. But the minute I decide a guy is all bad he
does some noble deeds that seem all out of character. Or the
very person I come to see as solid and trustworthy, suddenly
sells out his own mother or lets his children down."

Aside from the theoretical question of whether man is basically good or basically bad, which gets us nowhere since he is
both, it does seem unfortunate to me that religion has spent so
much of its time trying to convince people what great sinners
they are, only to turn around, as soon as they are "on the program" to insist that they demand of themselves that they be
super! We give them an injection of self-repudiation and self-
loathing; then we quickly insert in the other hip a shot of ac-
cepting-forgiving-saving instant love. If man asks us what to
expect next, we are likely to dodge the whole issue or leave
him with the impression that he has just inherited perfection,
emancipation, and all lovelier-than-anybody traits. At least, he
will likely have his confusion and his compulsions — and consequently his critical-of-others attitudes — increased.

He may well become one of the righteous in a classification
which says, "There are only two classes of people, the righteous and the unrighteous; and the righteous do the classifying."

What I am deploring most is the fact that somewhere along the line we have lost the art of challenging people without condemning them. We do not know how to console and encourage without being put in the role of whitewashing and watering down our insights into competent living.

MAN'S RIGHT TO BE HUMAN

In the process of trying to motivate people to move toward their potential, we have forgotten that near the heart of the Christian message of acceptance and love is the concept that human beings were born in finitude, will die incomplete, and have the right to be human (limited) in their own way. This does not mean that I am encouraging people to be slobs, to settle for inferiority or mediocrity. I wish full potentiality for every person, all he can become in this world.

In Jesus God became man. He did not demand of man that he become superman. Christians are urged to accept each other's humanness and distinctiveness, not to demand conformity (cf. Matt. 7 and Romans 14). Jesus took people as they were, associated with them, seemed to be comfortable with them. Wild-eyed Simon Peter, deceitful Judas, those who evoked his "Father, forgive them for they know not what they do" — all must have felt that He was with them in their attempts to be human.

George Christian Anderson in his delightful *Man's Right to be Human* tells of speaking to an audience of psychiatrists and non-medical people. A theological student asked him how he reconciled self-acceptance with religious beliefs that man is essentially wicked. "If everyone did as he wanted, how could we develop self-control?"[1] Anderson made clear that self-acceptance is not the same as self-satisfaction and that he was not arguing for our being satisfied with our immorality. He in-

---

1 George Christian Anderson, *Man's Right to be Human* (New York: William Morrow and Company, 1959), pp. 158-159.

sisted on moral responsibility and the importance of high goals and competence in living effectively.

Somehow this approach seems to be closer to where we live today. Camus has his Dr. Rieux in *The Plague* to say: "You know, I feel more fellowship with the defeated than with saints. Heroism and sanctity don't really appeal to me, I imagine. What interests me is being a man." [2] After quoting this Camus passage, a modern theologian, the Dean of Chapel at Denison University, Dr. David O. Woodyard, reminds us that we were not born human but become so by the decisions we make. He writes that what God is doing in the world is to make people human and that "we have a model for that in the Man who lived for others, whose life took the shape of concern and care for all that warps and distorts us ... Once [he, through the purposes and acts of God] has touched your heart you can't be indifferent to the cries of persons in need, you can't be idle and complacent as if history would run its own course to the benefit of man, you can't sit back absorbing all the good things of life without sharing them. You have got to identify the saving and healing possibilities in each moment and allow all that you are to be instrumental in their fulfillment." [3]

If this is being Christian or being human, or both, make mine two. I'd love to do the will of God by being the best kind of human being I could become and by creating the environment for others who are in my life space.

How, then, can we truly help each other to be the finest human beings possible? Are we talking of Jung's individuation, Maslow's self-actualizing, self-realization and self-fulfillment only? I don't think so. In time we may find more accurate terms. For the time being let us speak of selfhood, personhood,

---

2 Albert Camus, *The Plague,* trans. Stuart Gilbert (New York: The Modern Library, 1948), p. 231.
3 David O. Woodyard, *Living Without God Before God* (Philadelphia: The Westminster Press, 1968), pp. 70-71. See also Ross Snyder's *On Becoming Human* (Abingdon Press, 1967) for an excellent discussion of this same idea, that to be Christian is to be human in the best sense of the word.

wholeness, autonomy under God, wholesome relatedness to those we confront (including God). But all of this sounds cold and static. Why not say that we are trying to find ourselves in a loving relationship as human beings, for ourselves, for others, and for the future which includes God.

How, then? Who helps whom? What are the components of being, becoming, and being with others which constitute attaining "mature manhood, measured by nothing less than the full stature of Christ" (Eph. 4:13 NEB). This will constitute the remainder of this chapter. In fact, the remainder of this volume is an attempt to present a few of the facets of how Christian concepts relate to man's humanness and even encourage his humanness. As Woodyard says, "So providence comes upon us as a claim, as a calling to be part of what God is doing in the world to make human life more human." [4]

DEVELOP SELF-APPRECIATION

If we are really going to help ourselves and our fellow creatures we need to learn to *develop self-appreciation*.

This sounds like heresy if I ever saw it.

Really, I am not talking simply of self-understanding, self-acceptance, or self-affirmation. I refer to the human experience of feeling favorable to one's self. You don't have to think you are Einstein, Beethoven, Michelangelo, or Plato. You simply appreciate yourself in all of your uniqueness and with your distinctive qualities. Like what you see.

A chaplain in a general hospital who has fought his way through to emotional serenity told me that he found himself standing in front of his mirror shaving recently. For the first time in his life he could say out loud to the man in the mirror, "I like you." Why not? If you do not appreciate what you have, who will? I feel that too long we have talked of the self-

---

4 *Op. cit.*, p. 71.

image and the self-concept and even self-perception. The important thing is self-appreciation.

One of my counselees told of going to her clergyman for counseling. After she told her story, he said, "The best I can hear you, you hate yourself. Why? Do you know that God loves and likes you? If you hate yourself, you are against God, on the opposite side of the fence."

Why should you not appreciate your uniqueness? You were not supposed to be a carbon copy of someone else. God made you unique. Appreciate yourself. More than that, appreciate what you see in other people. That will cause them to appreciate themselves, at least, for the time being. Instead of worrying about our own halos let's try shining up our neighbors'.

In our culture we have talked a great deal about *love* and its importance in living together in this expanding hostile world. It is such "a many splendored thing" that we find it hard to define. If we start out to illustrate, or give examples, our range extends all the way from a kindly look to a man on a cross. Erich Fromm in his most valuable little book, *The Art of Loving,* tries to encompass love in such terms as giving one's self in "care, responsibility, respect, and knowledge," [5] which he says are common to all forms of love.

Far from quarrelling with Fromm, I would like to suggest that the human experience of *appreciation* is a characteristic of love which very much needs to be emphasized in addition to or as inherent in his "basic elements" in love.

If you look in the dictionary you will find such definitions of *appreciate* as "to feel a warmth of satisfaction and approval in regard to [anything]," "to esteem the full worth of," "to admire," "to be grateful for." Its opposite is to "depreciate," "run down," "low rate," "belittle," "think little of." Appreciation gets close to the heart of Christian love. We may *care for* another person in a very condescending and patronizing manner.

---

5 Erich Fromm, *The Art of Loving* (Harper and Row, Publishers, Inc., 1956), p. 22.

Even *respect* is often cold and distant. But appreciating is a warm, valuing, lifting up word. If someone says, "I really appreciate you," you begin to think that maybe you are worth something after all. All he would have to do to depreciate you is to look away from you or look by you.

Jesus often found Himself trying to get people to appreciate themselves by telling them that their heavenly Father felt this way about them. Look at the birds or the grass or the lilies of the field (Matt. 6:25-34). "Are not five sparrows sold for two pennies? And not one of them is forgotten before God. Why, even the hairs of your head are all numbered. Fear not; you are of more value than many sparrows" (Luke 12:6-7). It would seem, then, in a day of forgotten men and downtrodden masses that an important part of Christian ethics is the appreciation of each and every one of them by those of us who can. The good news of God is that He appreciates us. The ultimate base for self-appreciation is that we are appreciated.

The heart of a loving act must be that one person, by look, act, or mode of being, says to another, "I appreciate you in all of your uniqueness and as you are; I am not only willing for you to be you, but I value you and who you are." *There is something uplifting and attractive about people who can appreciate others and who appreciate themselves.*

On the other hand, there are few people who can stand to be around those who are always coming up with "the perfect squelch" or who resort to rudeness or sarcasm. We find it hard, even, to be around people who by their very silences tell us that we are not worth talking to, or do not have sense enough to appreciate what they have to say. Grace and love go out to our fellow human beings with openness and sincere regard. The same is true between God and man, both ways.

Had you ever thought of saying, "God, I really appreciate you, for being who You are and like You are to me. You are great. I really appreciate Your life"? That might be better than saying "Praise Ye the Lord" or "Our dear heavenly Father, we thank Thee." We have hidden behind clichés and traditional and museum words so long that we find it hard to love God in an honest, sincere, simple vocabulary. Maybe what we do when we mouth the usual prayers is imitate others whom we have heard pray. Imitations have serious limitations. They are expressions of the remembered, not the outflowing of the renewed and enlivened parts of our *now* personalities.

In this volume we will be talking of self-love and self-appreciation in very much the same sense. Here, however, we are trying to leap over the debris of theological junk and help man to develop, not merely a healthy self-concept, but a self-feeling and self-appreciation — not quite self-adoration or self-adulation — that will enable him to stand his ground "when things are at their worst" (Eph. 6:13 NEB).

Start Where You Are

A second way that we help people to be human is to *start where they are*. Some will no doubt think that this means that we are saying "Sink down to their level;" "Become sub-human;" "If you can't help them, join them." Others may wonder why I did not start with this as point Number One in techniques of helping ourselves and others. For a very simple reason, we must posit as the bedrock of our religious structure how we feel about self. After that, the question is: How do we start reaching out to things and others, to work, to power structures, to recreational situations, to people in crises, to criminals, to heroes and heroines, and "to one of the least of these my brethren" (Matt. 25:40).

There is an interesting passage in the Gospels which speaks of Jesus looking at the masses and responding at the gut level. "When he saw the crowds, he had compassion for them, because they were harassed and helpless, like sheep without a shepherd" (Matt. 9:36). Where the translation reads "he had compassion" the original language says he had feeling for them in his "intestine" or "bowels." It was not a "think in" or "pray in" or "love in"; it was actually a *feeling with* them so deeply that it was experienced in the viscera. Any religion that does not affect the viscera is too superficial to matter. We need some "feel ins" in our society in which people are willing to get together and feel deeply what it means to be the other.

Perhaps the best place to start in knowing where people are would be the popular music of today. Since the actual mood which can only be caught in hearing the music is absent, we will have to take only the words.

One of the most characteristic songs of our day is from the Broadway musical, *Golden Rainbow*. It is "I've Gotta Be Me." After admitting that he may be right or wrong, and that he can only be what he is, he (the singer) affirms: "I won't settle down, or settle for less, As long as there's half a chance that I can have it all! I'll go it alone, That's how it must be. I can't be right for somebody else if I'm not right for me!" [6]

I'm impressed. These moderns are in search of authenticity, of genuineness, of selfhood and of finding out who on earth we are. I'm impressed! Most of the people in our society are trying to decide where they can go for a vacation, how dry to make the martinis, and how to lay aside enough for security in the retirement period in case their number doesn't come up before then. It sounds to me as if these song writers, and singers, and participant listeners are sincerely interested in who they are, where they are going, who they can become, and what will become of them.

Getting with our generation is largely a matter of getting off our high horses of pretense and asking ourselves whether we had rather be a person or a performer, whether we want to *be* or to *be successful,* and whether we can trust ourselves to start where we are and become what we can become, so help us God.

---

6 From "I've Gotta Be Me," reprinted with permission of Damila Music, Inc., 40 West 55th Street, New York, N.Y. 10019.

I feel like saying to these young singers: "Don't yell at me 'I've gotta be me.' That is what God wants you to be. He is trying to help you to be human, not sub, nor ahuman, nor super, but a thoroughly sound, solid, spiritual person called *homo spiritualis,* a person who has *soul."*

One of the reasons people have such a hard time being human is that we come at them with so many formats, blue-prints, and systems. They have to fit the system. The system may be propriety, protocol, thriftiness, manners, grammar, morals or religious rituals. And, of course, we have to simplify life by codes, rules, folkways, and even traditional patterns of morals and religions. It is when the format or system becomes fixed and demanding, not allowing for individual spontaneity, that it cripples us. Then we arrogantly impose our system on others and require conformism, even equate conformity with good morals. The Apostle Paul as translated by J. B. Phillips says an appropriate thing on this subject: "Don't let the world around you squeeze you into its own mold, but let God remold your minds from within" (Rom. 12:2).[7]

We Christians often speak out against the systems (rules, customs, practices) of the world, those outside the folds of faith. Unfortunately, we have squeezed many of our own peo-ple into molds which are just as deadly (so far as real alive-ness to Spirit and to our fellow-man) as the customs in the market place. Every counselor sees good people crippled by their own goodness, their legalisms.

Recently, I read a dialogue between the late Jewish philo-sopher, Martin Buber, and the noted American psychologist, Carl Rogers. At one point they are comparing Buber's "I-Thou relationship" to Rogers' concept of "acceptance." Rogers makes clear that he refuses to see a mentally ill person, for example, as a *sick* person; rather primarily a *person.* He says, concern-ing the therapeutic relationship: "I feel a real willingness for

---

7 J. B. Phillips, *The New Testament in Modern English* (New York: The Macmillan Company, 1958).

this other person to *be what he is.* I call that 'acceptance'. . . . My meaning there is that I'm willing for him to possess the feelings he *possesses,* to hold the attitudes he holds, to be the person he is." [8]

This is receiving a person, confronting him, as he is, without prejudice (prejudging) and without demands. It is taking him as God gives him to us. Furthermore, we need to have the same attitude towards ourselves at any given moment. Start where we are.

There is a clue to good child rearing, as well as other interpersonal relations, in the Book of Proverbs: "Train up a child in the way he should go, and when he is old he will not depart from it" (22:6). What it really says in the original is that we train him up "in the way he is." Of course, a certain amount of "setting limits" has to be done, even with adults, but human beings are helped most in becoming their whole selves by people who are not afraid to trust them to unfold as the lily (see Chapter 14).

FACING UP TO REALITY

A third way we help ourselves and others is by *facing up to reality.*

If someone asks "What is reality?" the question must not be played down. Seeing things as they are is not easy. *We tend to see things as we are.* Only God sees reality accurately.

For example, is the pessimist the realist, or the optimist? A realist has been defined as the one who touches the wet paint to see if the sign, "Wet Paint," means what it says. Was Columbus a realist? Or Jesus Christ? Or Socrates? Or the astronauts, for that matter?

I can show from my counseling files the pathetic and tragic failures of people whose grasp of reality was faulty or who looked away from reality just long enough to run off the road.

---

8 Martin Buber, *The Knowledge of Man* (London: George Allen & Unwin Ltd., 1965), pp. 169-170.

A boy and girl are about to become parents but are not married. "We thought we would be the lucky ones," they gave as their explanation. Now they must face the possibilities of abortion, of marriage and becoming parents before they are ready for it, or of her spending some months in hiding and then putting the baby out for adoption. The reality they had hoped for was college and a happy, well-planned marriage.

A doctor has "fallen in love," he says, with a nurse half his age at the hospital. For years he has told his wife that he is not going to live all his life with her nagging and fighting. The five children are trying to solve their parents' marriage problem. One has attempted suicide; another is getting more and more nervous.

A junior in college has completed his 26th LSD trip. He is so nervous and disturbed that he has had to drop out of college. Now he does not know whether he will go back. Having created a mythical and illusory world of frequent turn-ons, he finds the real everyday world boring and humdrum. He wanted to be significant, outstanding — "the big tripper."

The business executive is missing more and more days from work and frightening himself by the power alcohol is getting over him. He refuses to go to Alcoholics Anonymous because people would find out that he has an alcohol problem. What he does not know is that his wife has already seen an attorney with divorce in mind. All of his associates except those who have the same problem, know he is alcohol dependent. He has many reasons for drinking excessively (he will tell you all of them and expect you to believe him), but he continues to sell short his freedom to choose between the difficult and the easy. Reality becomes worse and worse; self-responsibility decreases; he must conceal the facts by eight or ten shots of alcohol a day.

These are dramatic and crisis-laden situations but everyone of us has set himself back by neglecting to look at reality and make choices based upon facts.

We procrastinate and then get all tensed up over the dead-line. We eat unwisely and then deceive ourselves about why we gained weight — "something wrong with my glands" alibi. We do offensive things and then act like people are mean and self-ish because they withdraw from us. We find out that someone does not like us and make a federal case out of it, as if all peo-ple are not misunderstood or disliked at times, or as if there is something wrong with the world when we are not loved per-fectly. We get lonely and bored, as if it is someone else's duty to create our friendships or plan our recreation. Or we find ourselves spiritually bankrupt when we have refused to read, think, or talk about matters that relate to keeping ourselves sane and happy as human persons.

People need "realitating." All of us do. We need to realitate ourselves privately and to listen to one another more. It is not enough to withdraw into our gardens and manicure our private feelings.

Unfortunately, all too often we are like Elwood P. Dowd in the play, *Harvey,* who was confronted by the psychiatrists, "We all have to face reality, Dowd — sooner or later." His polite reply was: "Doctor, I wrestled with reality for forty years, and I am happy to state that I finally won out over it."

Reality is never overcome. It is lived with and coped with and adjusted to, even profited by in personality growth.

Its most painful aspects show up, though, when we clamor and cry for the easy and decry the difficult. We refuse pain and shun anxiety. In a nutshell this is at the heart of our refusal to face reality and to deal constructively with it. I am no addict of the strenuous, nor do I welcome pain. Masochism (or self-infliction) does not appeal to me. I certainly consider it un-christian. However, it is a well proven fact that no one grows and finds human life a permanently livable situation who does not learn to shake hands with the out-of-jointness of life. We must make peace with up-againstness feelings.

Reality is not all bad. It may be ecstatic and full of joy but not unless we find a working approach to sickness, meanness, frustration and the inhumanity of ordinary people.

It is interesting that in the last decade there has developed a type of helping people called "reality therapy," by two West Coast psychiatrists, William Glasser and his teacher, G. L. Harrington. Other similar approaches have been made by Albert Ellis, called "rational therapy," and O. Hobart Mowrer in "integrity therapy." All of these have attempted to do for therapy (counseling) what theologians have tried for fifty years— to get rid of "the devil theory of human motivation." It is one thing to say, "I could not help it; the devil made me do it." It is a very similar thing to say, "I did it because of my oedipal feelings or my unconscious strivings or my neurotic condition."

Glasser's approach is essentially that of refusing to listen to the "complaints" *(Portnoy's Complaint)* which elaborate the counselee's alibis for self-defeating behavior. He will do that endlessly under the coaching of a skilled, conventional, Freudian therapist. Glasser would say, "Tell me what your goals are. Are you willing to be responsible, How are you relating to other human beings? You want respect and love and worthwhileness: how do you propose to get them?" This is an oversimplification, of course, but the point is that he turns away from a primary emphasis on how we got that way. He helps us to learn to be uncomfortable in our irresponsibility. Reality therapists would say that we must learn to act in such a way that we give and receive love, a way that makes us feel worthwhile and causes others to feel the same. Such acts are right and good. Glasser insists that therapy "will be successful when they are able to give up denying the world and recognize that reality not only exists but that they must fulfill their needs within its framework." [9] I believe that both Moses and Jesus would agree with this.

While Glasser focuses mostly on the ethical, right and

9 William Glasser, M.D., *Reality Therapy* (Harper and Row, 1965), p. 6.

wrong, aspects of reality because his work is primarily with delinquents, we may apply reality orientation to many other facets of living.

Jesus was describing reality when He described a broad way and a narrow way of living — the broad leading to destruction (Matt. 7:13-14). Paul was doing the same when he said, "None of us lives to himself, and none of us dies to himself" (Rom. 14:7 RSV). Or better still in his famous remarks about being content with whatever state he was in: "In any and all circumstances I have learned the secret of facing plenty and hunger, abundance and want. I can do all things in him who strengthens me" (Phil. 4:12-13 RSV). James, in his very practical letter, points that wars and fighting among us come from our bad attitudes, our "passions that are at war in your members" (4:1 RSV). Or: "A man may think he is religious, but if he has no control over his tongue, he is deceiving himself; that man's religion is futile. The kind of religion which is without stain or fault in the sight of God our Father is: to go to the help of orphans and widows in their distress and keep oneself untarnished by the world" (Jas. 1:26-27 NEB). How realistic can you get!

It would seem then, that a large part of learning to live successfully is coping effectively with the real world. Putting up with the things that we cannot change without bitterness. Attacking problems that can possibly be solved. Reaching out to enjoy the enjoyable. Giving ourselves to causes that seem worthwhile. In the language of the day, *tuning in* on that which seems worth our attention, and *turning on* towards those people and causes which we can believe in. This is reality which is most constructive.

LIMITEDNESS PLUS TRANSCENDENCE

Closely related to "realitation" is the acceptance, by ourselves and others, of the *limitedness* of people. And hasten quickly to add *plus transcendence*.

Two problems lie close to the center of this aspect of our living. First we come at life with demands, with formats and blueprints, with perfectionism. Perhaps this error goes back as far as the ancient Greeks with their images of a perfect world. Plato had his *ontos on* (ideal world). His compatriots had a colossal faith in the fact that "knowledge is virtue." "Know thyself" was then, and is to millions of misguided people today, the prime requirement for being a good person.

What this adds up to, practically, is that the more we know the better we will be. If someone does not do what is right, explain to him more clearly what the situation is, enlighten him, educate him, and he will straighten out. If there is one thing that modern psychology and sociology have exposed, it is that men do not do right because they know what right is, or do wrong because they do not understand the right.

Modern psychology, modern theology, and especially modern existential philosophy knows that what makes man good is his attachments. He is what he loves. He *is* to the extent that he loves. Jesus said this best: "If a man loves me, he will keep my word" — not if he merely understands them, or is afraid to be disobedient, or would feel guilty if he fails. Social scientists speak of this as identification. In order to become truly human we must care about someone, love, draw near to, open to, get with another. Religion consists of getting with God and His children, our fellow-man.

Here we come to the heart of what I am trying to say about man in his limitedness plus transcendence.

I have said that we have to start with people where they are. Now I wish to remind myself and others that we cannot live comfortably (with ourselves and others) unless we come to grips with and accept fully our own limitations.

Adam and Eve didn't like it (their fenced-in-ness). I don't like it. Most thoughtful people don't like it. It is an attack on our grandiose ideas, wishes, and dreams. We do not like the risk of being wrong so we develop our dogmatisms, our clos-

ures. We hate uncertainty so we ask God to give us unequiv-
ocal answers, or we deny freedom and profess faith in fate, de-
terminism, predestination, or look for explanations in astrology
— the truth is, we do not know why things happened as they
did in the past or what will happen in the future.

We cannot stand to be weak, so we develop hypocrisy,
pretend to be stronger than we are. We find it hard to admit
our doubts, so we over profess certainty. We do not like to
make the wrong decisions, so we procrastinate. We despise our
limited knowledge, the fact of our ignorance, so we become
rigid and intolerant in order to prevent any challenge of our
finitude. We insist that we have only one feeling about our
friend, our parent, or our child (no ambivalence, no two feelings). This prevents our admitting that we are human.

The sad fact about such black and white, all or none,
super-human, attitudes is that it separates us from our fellow
human beings, causes us to play phoney roles, and develops
within us a kind of grandiosity which at the worst may lead to
insanity and at the best will prevent integrity or growth.

We need to join the human race. We have to learn to live
with uncertainty, ambiguity, risk, insecurity, and ambivalence,
even with the absurd.

This may sound to many as if I am saying that we must resist trying to be superhuman, settle down to tyranny and hypocrisy, the stink and rats of the slums, the stupidities and ignorance all about us, and do nothing. Not at all. I am saying that
there is place for failure and puzzlement in life but that something in man butts his head against this and defies it. This I
admire.

Here we have transcendence. Camus states this beautifully
in an essay which he wrote in 1944: "Nothing is given to men,
and the little they can conquer is paid for with unjust deaths.
But man's greatness lies elsewhere. It lies in his decision to be
stronger than his condition. And if his condition is unjust, he

has only one way to overcome it, which is to be just himself."[10]

Jesus sounded a similar but more certain note (maybe that is why he has had such a profound influence through 1900 years): "I have said this to you, that in me you may have peace. In the world you will have tribulation; but be of good cheer, I have overcome the world" (John 16:33 RSV).

In this passage we have two words which represent the poles of human life: "tribulation," which is a Greek word meaning "pressed together," and the word "be of good cheer," which really says, "Be bold or be confident."

Man has strange ways of feeling trapped and at the same time feeling that there must be some way out. He does not accept the human condition as inevitable. He rises above it.

Let me give you an example. A very morose medical student (female) had spent ten years in a devastating marriage. Now she had gotten out. Suspicions, wounds, self-images, made up her repertoire of traits and feelings. What did she do? At one point she decided to quit scapegoating and become the kind of human being who could turn her back on the past and brave the future with a new outlook. She moved on. Her focus became different. Her deep feelings of love and trust and hope projected her into the future. She transcended her past.

Numerous examples could be given.

There is something in human beings which makes them rise up and move out to new horizons. Man is a creature of expansion, of enlargement, of overcoming. Who knows where he is going next? "Build thee more stately mansions, O my soul."

Take Mt. Everest for example. In 1963 from February to June, a 17-member team ranging in age from 26 to 44 climbed the 29,028 foot mountain. Four were Ph.D's, three held M.D. degrees, three were Masters, and all but one of the rest had bachelor's degrees. Fifteen were married, two for the second time, and only three were childless.

---

10 Albert Camus, *Resistance, Rebellion, and Death* (New York: Alfred A. Knopf, Inc., 1960), pp. 39-40.

Why did these people climb Mt. Everest? They had to! It is the Tower of Babel story over again (Gen. 11:1-11). People have to rise.

Or take the three men who made the moon trip: Armstrong, Aldrin, and Collins. Why did they take these terrific chances? They had to. Why did all the world stand up and help them? Not pure science. There is something in man that makes him defy boundaries. Man has some kind of yen to transcend, to explore, to go beyond.

Now we have a new address. Our view of heaven as *up* is passé. Our understanding of the universe must change. Heaven is not up. Jesus is not "out there," but "in here" and "with you."

One of the best portrayals of this change in our conception of where we are is in Thornton Wilder's play, *Our Town*.

He has Rebecca, one of the characters, tell of a minister who has written a letter to a girl in Grover's Corners, New Hampshire, and instead of leaving the address that simple, he goes much beyond the obvious. The address reads:

> Jane Crofut,
> The Crofut Farm,
> Grover's Corners,
> Cutton County,
> New Hampshire,
> United States of America,
> Continent of North America,
> Western Hemisphere,
> The Earth,
> The Solar System,
> The Universe,
> The Mind of God.

We will not be satisfied until we are better acquainted with the Mind of God. Who are we kidding? We can know the Mind of God only as He has chosen, and chooses, to make Himself known (Phil. 2:5-11). To be human is to be terribly limited so far as knowing God is concerned, as well as knowing what the moon, and Mars and the rest of out there is concerned.

Transcendence, however, coupled with the acknowledgment of our limitedness, is a part of the human condition. By this (transcendence) we as human beings rise; without it we fall.

I should like to summarize what I have tried to say in this chapter in two quotations.

Dr. Lawrence S. Kubie, noted psychiatrist, has written: "It is a difficult and complex thing to be a human being, and the human race is not up to it yet. Part of the capacity to be a human being is the capacity of one human being to love another. This is a peculiarly human challenge." [11]

An equally well-known psychologist, Dr. A. H. Maslow, says: "On the whole I think it fair to say that human history is a record of the ways in which human nature has been sold short. The highest possibilities of human nature have practically always been underrated. Even when 'good specimens,' the saints and sages and great leaders of history, have been available for study, the temptation too often has been to consider them not human but supernatually endowed." [12]

I personally believe that Jesus really was unique, supernaturally endowed, but that is my private business. Nevertheless, I join hands with all men everywhere who are trying to help all men everywhere to become more human — not sub, not half, not super, and certainly not inhuman.

---

11 Chapter II, "Psychoanalysis and Marriage," in *Neurotic Interaction in Marriage,* ed. Victor W. Eisenstein, M.D. (New York: Basic Books, Inc., 1956), p. 43.
12 Article: "Toward a Humanistic Biology," *American Psychologist,* Vol. 24, No. 8 (Aug. 1969), p. 726.

CHAPTER TWO

Tell It Like You See It

There is something urgent and longing about many of the modern popular songs. They are straightforward. They are not fooling around. They reach out for life with an immediacy that stabs you and makes you ask yourself serious questions.

Many of today's songs on the surface are concerned with seduction, but aside from that, there are evidences that young people want to slash through the game-playing and the unreality of pretense. They are stalking out into the open almost naked and unashamed.

There is a kind of Nietzschean quality about words that exclaim that life is too short for sorrow, words that command, "Go on and live, baby."

I wonder if this is not very close to what Christianity at its best has been saying to people. Get with reality. Live. Tell it like it is. Here is self-trust, acting from within, looking hard at alternatives, searching for what seems real — all tied up in one bundle of life.

Moses thrust this same set of alternatives in the face of the Israelites: "I call heaven and earth to record this day against you, that I have set before you life and death, blessing and cursing: therefore choose life, that both thou and thy seed may live" (Deut. 30:19).

Jesus sounded the same note when he said, "I have come that men may have life, and may have it in all its fullness" (John 10:10 NEB).

31

What Religion Is All About

It is time in this day, when there is such questioning about the relevance of the Church and even of the Bible, to ask ourselves (with Alfie), "What is it all about?"

This may seem a strange question to some people who have grown up in the midst of Sunday school and in a family which read the Bible and talked about religion. Granted, this is a small percent of our population. Most people do not know the Bible "from nothing," and could care less.

Why is this? Why do people smile if you expect them to know whether a particular quotation is from Shakespeare, Alexander Pope, Benjamin Franklin, or from the Bible?

There are two big reasons, it seems to me. First the Church, in its Bible teaching and preaching, has placed so much emphasis on museum and archaeological aspects of religion and missed the real life impact of Bible stories. Arguments over whether there really was an Adam and Eve, about the validity of Noah's ark or the lion's den story in Daniel, or whether Jesus actually fed 5,000 people at once from a boy's lunch basket, or even whether the graphic descriptions in Revelation represent literal prophecy of a historic time table — such discussion leaves modern man cold. These seem so far from the nitty-gritty issues at the office or on the weekend trip to the cabin at the lake.

The average John and Jane Doe are like the little boy who was fighting having to go to Sunday school. His argument was, "Why should I go down there and study about a lot of old people who I have never met and probably never will meet?"

The other big reason why so much aversion has accumulated against traditional religion is the way its teachings — whether Bible centered or church council centered — have been used to condemn, scare, threaten, and coerce.

Modern man is not easily frightened; he knows the group scare techniques used by the Hitlers and blackmailers. He inherently knows that God, if there is a God, would not use the I'm-bigger-than-you-so-knuckle-under technique, or resort to the psychologically torturous concept of you're-gonna-get-it-in-the-end approach.

Take the Ten Commandments. Even a superficial reader can see how remote, fuzzy and useless some of them are to modern life. Some preachers almost produce a hernia trying to drag them into the twentieth century. Who believes in working six days? Or where are the graven images we are not to make? Honoring father and mother gets all mixed up when, due to divorce, you have had four fathers and two of them were alcoholic. Adultery is even more vague when you try to distinguish it from heavy petting or homosexuality. And in a culture where buying becomes a duty, what does "Thou shalt not covet" mean? The opposite to the Tenth Commandment has become a Golden Rule in this day that taboos cash and encourages credit purchasing. If we really mean that we are to love God and our neighbors, establish our own value systems, observe territoriality, relate to one another as whole persons, not just sexually, why don't we tell it like it is?

Modern man, to use that cliché again, is sick and tired of religionists coming up with closed systems of morals and truth, especially in archaic language — king of kings, justification, sanctification, and even covenant — and refusing to allow adventuring and thoughtfully exploring new ways to confess our faith or practice the loving life.

What is religion all about, then? It is about life, how to *love* it. It is about an alleged unveiling or disclosing of the Supreme Being, not just in the past but contemporaneously. It is about who we are and what we can *become*. It concerns relationships, how we contact one another (and God), and how we keep in touch. It is about finding ourselves, managing ourselves, and giving ourselves to that which will mean to us stability and significance.

It is not intellectualizing about God or man, the usual meaning of doctrine. It must be more than do's and don'ts, ethics, codes, systems of accepted patterns of behavior. It is not merely private or public rituals such as prayer, Bible reading, singing, or taking communion, as valuable as these may be at times.

Religion is experiencing self, our fellow-man, God, as we go about the precarious business of living a life. Theology or God-talk, as John Macquarie calls it, is trying to talk intelligently about God as we understand Him, and all of the things He is doing in, around, to, and through us.

WHO AM I? WHO IS GOD?

A baby born into the world does not know who he is. In fact he gradually finds out, we do not know exactly how, when, and through what precise instrumentations. It is through his interaction with others that he comes to be known to himself and to others.

So the meaning of faith is that we get glimpses of the One who has no adequate name except "I will be what I will be." He speaks to man in a garden, at Mt. Sinai, at the backside of the desert, under a juniper tree, by the road from Jerusalem to Jericho, in a Roman prison. In the history of men, to this list of the ways God makes Himself felt to man could be added the starry heavens above, Schubert's "Unfinished Symphony."

We could say a lot of clichéd things about the Bible becoming the normative word of God, serving as guide or standard for our interpretation of God, who He is and what He is doing. The catch phrase here is the word, "interpretation of God." It sounds too intellectual. It is response to God that is aimed at. Perhaps to talk of God's speaking to us, as Tillich claimed, is symbolic language. We can hardly avoid it, however. The sunset or the poem or the drama may speak to us. Or, for that matter, so may the eight murders in the beauty shop at La

Mesa, Arizona, or the Negro ghetto, or the alcoholic, and the homosexual.

Man experiences himself as one who is capable of being spoken to. Whether or not we believe that there is a God who speaks, we cannot avoid knowing ourselves as listeners, responders, initiators of acts, perpetrators of crimes, creators of empires, crusaders, saviors and sadists.

Take that dramatic story in the first of the Bible, the Creation. It is saying that we sprang from both dust and deity, that we are thrust into a situation of choice, that we need relationships but get lost because we forget who we are or reject our dependent state and get estranged. The tower of Babel, the history of Israel and the Parable of the Wicked Husbandmen (Matt. 21), all tell essentially the same story, that man is a creature who looks heavenward but gets hung up in his involvement about himself. He tries to be God.

If we would forget the literal details of the Bible stories (like how long Methuselah lived, or the size and air-conditioning of Jonah's whale), we might see that religion is trying to tell who we are, what may become of us, and what we might become — a little less than God (Ps. 8:5).

If we would tell it like it is in the Bible, and not get entrapped in name calling like King of Kings, Prince of Peace, Savior, Messiah, lost, sinner, saint, and saved we might catch a glimpse of the fact that the overall meaning of the Bible is who God is, how He acts, who we are and how we may be enabled to behave.

NEARNESS VERSUS DISTANCE

A second pivotal point that the Christian faith is dealing with is *nearness versus distance*. For that matter, so is the Jewish religion.

Religion easily falls back into thinking in terms of an absentee God, living under God, behind God's back, or even as the Supreme Being as a kind of mysterious originator of things and persons (in that order). Modern theologians try to get closer to the religious experience by speaking of our seeing ourselves *before* God.

The true experience of the man of faith must be characterized by one word, *nearness*. All of us know what the feeling of nearness is. We have been in a crowded street and felt a thousand miles from anyone, or sitting beside a worshiper in a church and experiencing distressing distancing. Husbands and wives have told me repeatedly of how they never felt close to each other even in the same bed. Teenagers lament, "I cannot get close to my daddy."

Relationship or confrontation, which is so often held out as the salvation of modern man, is more than being in sight of, being signed up on the same roster, or even living next door. Proximity does not bring either peace or power. It may bring a sword. Even sex does not bring closeness, to many people.

Spiritual or psychological nearness is the essence of the faith life.

Ever since Adam and Eve hid themselves from the presence of the Lord God, men have been alternating between the poles of nearness and distance (both poorly defined). Nearness is not symbiosis or personality fusion or some sort of self-obliterating togetherness. Rather it is communion, a harmony and warmth and unity of persons of spirits which respond with favor and acceptance to each other.

Great slogan-like, loaded passages which highlight this experience of nearness are well known: Psalm 139 in which the writer despairs of finding any place inside himself or in the universe where the Lord is not — "Whither shall I flee from thy presence?" Isaiah 55:6 says, "Seek ye the Lord while he may be found, call ye upon him while he is near." The non-religious people of Jesus' day felt the drawing power of the and warmth and unity of persons of spirits which respond with Master, "Then drew near unto him all the publicans and sinners for to hear him" (Luke 15:1). "Come to me." Jesus kept saying, "...and learn from me, for I am gentle and humble in spirit; and you will find rest" (Matt. 11:28-29 TEV). Paul in a speech on Mars Hill in Athens boldly declared that God is "not far from every one of us" (Acts 17:27). James in his letter wrote, "Draw nigh to God, and he will draw nigh to you" (4:8).

Meister Eckhart, who lived in the last half of the 13th and the first quarter of the 14th centuries, knew how to become aware of the nearness of God. He wrote:

> I am as sure of this as I am that I am alive: nothing is as near to me as God is. God is nearer to me than I am to myself. My being depends on God's intimate presence. So, too, He is near to a stick or a stone but they do not know it. If the stick knew God and recognized how near he is, as the holy angels know such things, the stick would be as blessed as angels .... Man is more blessed because God is in him and so near that he has God — but in that he is aware of how near God is, and knowing God, he loves him.
>
> ... God is equally near to everything and every place and is equally ready to give himself, so far as in him lies, and therefore a person shall know him aright who knows how to see him the same, under all circumstances.[1]

Whether we call God our nearest kinsman, feel Him closer than the artery in our neck, or sing about "My God and I" walking the fields together, we are trying to say that the act of faith is experiencing nearness and the acts of sin are distancing in one form or another. "Nearer, My God, to Thee" is a hymn that will likely last for many years like the popular songs, "Near You" and "Tenderly."

> Speak to Him thou for He hears, and
> Spirit with Spirit can meet —
> Closer is He than breathing, and nearer
> than hands and feet.
>
> TENNYSON

---

1 *Meister Eckhart,* trans. by Raymond Bernard Blakney (New York: Harper Torchbooks, Harper & Row, 1941), pp. 129-30.

If we were to abandon some of our traditional formal terms like repentance, confession, belief, accepting Christ as Savior, and come right to the heart of the matter of knowing God through Christ, if we were to tell it like it is, we would have to say that religion is not just calling on God or calling out to our fellow-man, but drawing near.

STABILIZING RELATIONSHIPS

A third action of religion is to stabilize relationships. This does not imply a status quo or a static condition. Life flows. Personalities change, even crumble and fragment. People in relatedness vacillate back and forth, even turn their backs on each other at times. God, we believe, is different. It is interesting that the same terms that are used about interaction between God and man are the ones used about man's ways of relating to man.

Revelation or self-disclosure is absolutely necessary to getting to know one another, else we guess at one another. Covenant, an archaic sounding word, really means an agreement and rests upon a kind of predictability of a person. Faith is meeting on reliable grounds. Repentance is getting a new mind, seeing things differently after the failure, and re-relating (forgiveness) after strain or estrangement.

Or take the most common words which are used to describe how broken and estranged man comes to find himself redeemed. *Redemption* means setting free, as from a debtor's prison or from enslavement. If we mean freedom, why do we not tell it like it is instead of hiding behind a word which has come to apply mainly to S & H Green Stamps, and say what we are freed from, and what we are freed to do and be — perhaps to love and to act from within in joyous spontaneity. *Salvation* involves two very important life-involvement ideas: healing of illness (wholeness) and deliverance. Who can look around himself, or within, and not observe ravaging illnesses and crippling bondages? *Justification* means acceptance in spite of our unacceptibility, and issuing in continued and developing co-operation on the part of man, who has not heretofore felt the gracious behavior (grace) of God.

Even *regeneration* (the new birth) and *conversion* may be quibbled over by intellectualizers, but actually it is not an over-simplification to see it as "an individual happening" which grows out of an act of God. It is what man allows God to do when he starts all over, *new* — a key word in the New Testament.

All of these brief statements are but an earnest attempt to say that religion is about man's life, in experiencing what he calls God. The tendency now to talk of a religionless Christianity and to relate to God only as we see Him in our fellow-man does not greatly disturb me. I see it as man's attempt to bypass the abstract clutter of such terms as omniscience, omnipotence, omnipresence, original sin (which never seems too original), and even existentialism — to come to look at the "unique, unrepeatable person and the unique, unrepeatable situations" (Buber).

In other words, the world will not stand still. People in these unique, unrepeatable (no two alike) situations leave us wondering whether we may find ourselves out in left field with all the other players gone home and the bleachers empty. What can we expect from such men in such a world? If there is a God, how does He provide our limitedness with some semblance of assurance?

Here is where the good news (translation of the word *gospel*) comes in. The only thing consoling in a constantly changing world is relatedness. God loves us — that sounds phoney and sentimental, but I know of no other way to say it — and we can rely on that. People love us, I would like to say, but that is not always true. Those who can, do. The others provide us with an unbounding opportunity to show "grace and truth," love and realistic living.

This is what we need, love, and an opportunity to be loving. In such a relationship we can find stability.

Three people who have gone to church all of their lives were in dialogue with me recently about their church and religion.

One said, "I would enjoy going to church more if the preachers would stick to the Word and quit talking about social problems. Our young people need to be told that God has commandments and if they do not keep them they will be punished. There are still some eternal verities, you know."

A rather closely reasoned discussion which followed revealed that this person believed in a religion of fear and threats and psychological blackmail, that we ought to obey God because He is bigger than we are, and in the end, we will have to bow down or be demolished. By the Word she meant selecting passages which would either explain ideas or concepts or harping on commandments such as the ones about adultery, church attendance and tithing. By "eternal verities" she referred to what she called "laws" of the spirit such as selfishness leading to unhappiness and self-indulgence destroying our ability to control ourselves. I guess she is partly right. However, her viewpoint seemed a long way from Paul's "All who are led by the Spirit of God are sons of God" (Rom. 8:14 RSV); or Jesus' calling people to know God by coming to Him.

The second conversation was with a young priest in the Roman Catholic Church and a college professor, a Lutheran layman. As we talked of how attitudes were changing toward guilt and fear of punishment and even fear of disgrace, the young priest and I were examining the new motives which must be sought to help people want to live for God and their fellowmen. We hardly expected religious jargon from a layman. Here is what he said, "We do not need scare techniques to motivate people. Feeling bad is not the reason for doing good. I find it a joy to witness to my fellow faculty members. Some of them look at me like I must be joking. To me religion is exciting

and joyous. Living the Christian life does not have to be a
drag. If there is a better way of living than following the living
Christ I would like to find it. I don't believe all of the junk that
some people have tried to saddle on me, but I still believe in
Christ and Christian fellowship."

The third one was a counselee of mine who said, "I go to
church but the preachers seem to talk about things that do not
involve my everyday problems. I'm a divorcee, as you know.
Why don't pastors help us to know how to reconcile the
church's doctrines with the fact that I have failed in two mar-
riages and do not know whether to live single, which I don't
think I can do without sex, or try another marriage. I get the
feeling when I hear a sermon, or even in a Sunday school class,
that the church leaders are talking about their highflown doctrines because they are afraid to get down to where most people live and wrestle with our problems. Am I being too critical?"

I never answered the question. I did not know what she
had been hearing. There are church leaders who are determined to tell it like it is, to make religion relevant to daily living, to allow Christ to speak to the marketplace. We do not
know where we are going in the modern church. Thank God.
We may find leadership under these circumstances. Those who
are not willing to live in uncertainty — and walk by faith —
must go ahead living in sin, the sin of being in a rut, with a
philosophy and a system as an idol.

RELIGION IS FINDING MEANING

Besides seeing the life of faith in Christ as being about the
loving life, about who we are as selves, about drawing near,
and relationships, we see that it is about how we find meaning
or significance.

It is possible to live and die without finding anything to
live for or worth dying for. Life is like a cat chasing his tail or

a bird nesting, mating and migrating; then doing it all over again next spring.

Homo sapiens is homo ludens (man of happiness) also, and this species looks for some kind of inner feeling that he is *getting with* something good in life. It may not make sense but it makes significance. Your spirit is elevated by the feeling that you may not be the greatest but you are somebody and worthwhile. You feel that you matter.

D. H. Lawrence wrote in his *The Man Who Died* (a short novel about Christ): "For men and women alike were mad with the egoistic fear of their own nothingness." They were and are. Who has not asked himself in the middle of the night or while riding along by himself in a car: What does my being here mean? Does it matter very much what I do? What will become of me? What is worth giving my time and attention to? What is really important in life? Asking these questions may drive us mad if somewhere in the process we decide to do nothing but think and talk. Talking may lead to substituting words for action, like the person who hallucinates substitutes his mental images for the physical world out there.

Jesus probably meant for His disciples to take seriously and make central His words: "Whoever is willing to do what God wants will know whether what I teach comes from God or whether I speak on my own authority" (John 7:17 TEV). To get open to working with God, even though you may not agree with all of the Church's creeds or programs, brings a kind of self-authenticating conviction. Don't ask me to explain this. It just does. When you let God use you in finding jobs for poor people, in sitting with the aged, or teaching a Bible class, or whatever "God wants you to do," it brings about an assuring meaningfulness.

This is what Jesus meant by the kingdom or reign of God. Apparently the expression "kingdom of God" was on His lips repeatedly.

I see again and again in our day something like those young men in Palestine were seeking in Jesus' day. Young people *are* seeking the kingdom of God and His rightness or fairness (Matt. 6:33).

Why are they marching in protests which, in most cases, can get them nothing but a black mark on their future record? Why have they joined the Peace Corps and Vista and other service groups? Even the hippies, many of them, are seeking the kingdom of God, a world nearer to what makes for justice and love. I have known some who talked about their experiences in meditation very much as the early Church did, after Pentecost. When they see one another as "beautiful people," and have the courage to turn their backs on the kingdoms of big business, fame, security, and material comforts, they are seeking something. It may be the kingdom of God.

I have a feeling that many young people today are saying the same thing to our generation as the young man, John the Baptist, and the young man, Jesus, and His apostles were saying to their generation. "The kingdom of heaven is at hand." "The kingdom of God is within you." "Seek first his kingdom and his righteousness, and all these things will be yours as well." Jesus stood up in His home town synagogue and re-announced Isaiah's prediction: "He has sent me to announce good news to the poor, to proclaim release for prisoners and recovery of sight for the blind, to let the broken victims go free." This sounds like a presidential platform. Then he said, "Today in your hearing this text has come true." Today! He was a Now person.

The news and interview and panel shows on TV are talking of poverty marches, finding jobs for ex-cons, new medicines for the recovery of the mentally ill, restoring the alcoholic, the prevention of crime in our cities, the manpower training programs, peace corpsmen projects and a world of rehabilitations and restorations and "realitations." The kingdom of heaven is coming near.

I am not for a moment equating the reign of God with a particular health, economic, or educational program. What I am saying is that the radical, at times fanatical, thrust of many people toward a better world, toward an attacking of man's inhumanity to man, is very much like a "hunger and thirst after righteousness." People who have a dream, even an "impossible dream," are living. They find meaning.

There are many ways that modern man attacks this menace of meaninglessness. He may become a cog in a great, big, rolling, revolutionizing wheel. He may isolate himself in an attic and create a picture or write a story. He may push the cleaning machine down a hospital corridor and know that he is helping care for patients. Or he may write ad copy in a public relations firm. It is God's world. The line of distinction between the secular and the sacred has become dim or completely obliterated.

Piet Hein, the Danish poet, had a perspective which could dignify any job or give meaning to the most insignificant life, in his poem "Simply Assisting God":

> I am a humble artist
> molding my earthly clod,
> adding my labor to nature's,
> simply assisting God.
>
> Not that my effort is needed;
> yet somehow, I understand,
> my maker has willed it that I too should have
> unmolded clay in my hand.[2]

Maybe our problem of finding meaning is not new. Perhaps we are simply more aware of it because of cybernetics and because the spiritual or psychological man is emerging. At least, modern religion has the chance of a lifetime to help us overcome the fear of our nothingness.

---

2 Piet Hein, *Grooks 1* (Cambridge, Mass.: M.I.T. Press, 1966), p. 7.

The revolt of the human spirit against cynicism and nihilism is portrayed perfectly in Katherine Anne Porter's *Ship of Fools.* Toward the end of the book, the ship's captain is attempting to persuade Dr. Schumann to give up his idea of going off into exile with a woman who is being deported, and with whom he had found love during the voyage. Schumann is the ship's doctor, and is going home to his wife and two sons.

Dr. Schumann says, "I dreamed that I died and was in my closed casket, and when the realization came to me that it was all over, I pounded on the casket screaming and knowing that my life couldn't be over — because I had never lived." [3] I have never lived! Pathetic words!

The Christian faith holds out one big thing to people — life. It is life that feels like life, that rises above the absurd aspects of living, that finds meaning in *being,* not merely in doing or going some place.

Now that I have come to the end of this chapter and have repeated the theme, "Tell it like it is," I feel embarrassed. No one ever really does that. Only God could. We do not know how it is. The best any of us can do is to tell it like we see it. Perhaps like we feel it or sense it or hope it. The human race might learn to live together in peace and respect if more people could hear each other, even when we talk about the good news of God, when we honestly and simply try to tell it like we see it. I vote for that!

---

3 Katherine Anne Porter, *Ship of Fools* (Boston: Little, Brown and Company, 1962).

CHAPTER THREE

Love Versus Hate

The people who are "clothed in their right minds" these days are worried about whether we are going to survive. We are like a little boy who climbs into an automobile and steps on the starter, only to find that a machine that he does not know how to drive is moving away with him. It is high time that we do a more realistic job of finding out what is wrong with our world. We cannot kid ourselves about the potential disaster of nuclear warfare, or our pollution of our natural resources, or the constantly rising cost of living. These are not at the heart of our problem. When we discuss our group problems, we do as the average individual does when he is trying to get at his own personal problem — we lack one step going far enough.

For example, man says science has created a juggernaut that is about to crush him. But that is not necessarily so. Science is a servant, just as governmental systems and factories and schools and all other institutions are servants. In war, science kills men by explosives and also saves their lives by medicine. It builds bridges and blows them up. It allays fevers and spreads germs. It inflicts pain and deadens the nerves that transmit it. Science is neither saint nor demon; it is a slave.

Where, then, are we to lay the blame for the condition of our world? On science? On nationalism? On capitalism? No, all of these are one step removed from the real difficulty.

And a wrong diagnosis at this point may lead us to Armageddon, to a final conflagration that shall destroy us all.

Dr. Karl Menninger, of the famous Menninger Clinic at Topeka, said:

> The psychologist, speaking for science, is like a voice crying in the wilderness. "The disease of the world is the disease of the individual personality," he says. No one listens. "The World War of today is a reflection of multiple miniature wars in the hearts of individuals," he persists. He is met with silence. "The war of nations is a magnification of the war of human instincts, human motives," he cries. "What of it?" someone asks.[4]

Does that sound like strange talk to you? It is what Jesus and His apostles preached to the world almost two thousand years ago. It may be expressed best in the words of our Master, "Man shall not live by bread alone, but by every word that proceedeth out of the mouth of God" (Matt. 4:4).

THE CONFLICT BETWEEN LOVE AND HATE

Let us get to the very heart of the matter: our world is involved in a conflict between love and hate. As long as hate wins, we will continue to have wars — perhaps eventually complete destruction. If love wins, we might build a world of peace and prosperity such as the Utopia builders have never dared dream. But wait! What has been said about our world may be said also of our homes, our churches, our schools — about every group enterprise; all our relationships all over the world.

Not long ago two men got into a fight; one cut the other's throat. Hate had won. A couple went before a judge and said that the vows they had taken at the altar were already broken and that they did not wish to live together any longer. Hate

---

4 Karl Menninger, *Love Against Hate* (New York: Harcourt, Brace & World, Inc., 1942), p. 4.

had overcome love again. Some church leaders and their pastor had such violent conflict that, as a result, some members of
the church refused to speak to one another, and some talked
in a strained and distrustful manner, while others called one
another bad names and even talked of fighting physically. Hate
had won again.

One of the most difficult tasks that a preacher has, or any
other person who is trying to deal realistically with human
problems, is to get people to see how natural hate is in human
life. We don't like to admit our destructiveness, or we call it by
other names and deceive ourselves. I do not know why we put
up such a strenuous fight to fool ourselves, unless it is that
when we admit the truth about ourselves we just cannot stand
ourselves.

WHAT THE BIBLE SAYS ABOUT HATE

But here the Bible ought to help us. Do you know that the
Bible is extremely frank on the subject of human hate? It is as
if God is saying to man: "You don't have to hide your true self
from Me any longer, for I know all about the deep reservoir of
hate down in your mind, and I sent my Son to save you from
it. You don't have to pretend to be all love."

Note these passages from the New Testament:

> You have heard that it was said, "You shall love your
> neighbor and hate your enemy." But I say to you, Love your
> enemies and pray for those who persecute you, so that you
> may be sons of your Father who is in heaven; for he makes his
> sun rise on the evil and on the good, and sends rain on the
> just and on the unjust. For if you love those who love you,
> what reward have you? Do not even the tax collectors do the
> same? And if you salute only your brethren, what more are
> you doing than others? Do not even the Gentiles do the same?
> You, therefore, must be perfect, as your heavenly Father is
> perfect (Matt. 5:43-48 RSV).

And he [Jesus] said, That which cometh out of the man, that defileth the man. For from within, out of the heart of men, proceed evil thoughts, adulteries, fornications, murders, thefts, covetousness, wickedness, deceit, lasciviousness, an evil eye, blasphemy, pride, foolishness: all these evil things come from within, and defile the man (Mark 7:20-23).

If the world hate you, ye know that it hated me before it hated you. If ye were of the world, the world would love his own; but because ye are not of the world, but I have chosen you out of the world, therefore the world hateth you (John 15:18-19).

Now the works of the flesh are manifest, which are these, Adultery, fornication, uncleanness, lasciviousness, idolatry, witchcraft, hatred, variance, emulations, wrath, strife, seditions, heresies, envyings, murders, drunkenness, revelings, and such like: of the which I tell you before, as I have also told you in time past, that they which do such things shall not inherit the kingdom of God. But the fruit of the Spirit is love, joy, peace, long-suffering, gentleness, goodness, faith, meekness, temperance: against such there is no law (Gal 5:19-23).

For we ourselves also were sometimes foolish, disobedient, deceived, serving divers lusts and pleasures, living in malice and envy, hateful, and hating one another (Titus 3:3).

We know that we have passed from death unto life, because we love the brethren. He that loveth not his brother abideth in death. Whosoever hateth his brother is a murderer: and ye know that no murderer hath eternal life abiding in him (1 John 3:14-15).

Hatred is one of the early emotions of the infant. It is probably the second emotion that each of us experienced, the first being fear. Rebecca West, in a magnificent chapter in *Living Philosophies,* concedes that "hatred necessarily precedes love in human experience." She assumes that it is "an early error of the mind, which becomes a confirmed habit before reason can disperse it." The truth is probably that we do not learn to hate or to get angry; we come into this world equipped for aggression and destruction. All of us know that when two children are put in a play pen together, before long they may bite each other, pull hair, or rob each other of toys. Such behavior patterns are very common in childhood; that is why both Christian people and others talk about the hate way of life as immature and the love way as adult. We know that it is hard to grow up and love people; it is so much easier to hate and fight and be bitter. That is why the world is so full of sorrow and bitterness and resentment and injustice.

How We Express Hate

Consider now how hate expresses itself. Some will not like the term "hate"; but call it hostility, antagonism, aggression, destructiveness, or whatever you will, it is a part of the same reaction. Hate is an attempt or tendency to hurt, to make unhappy, or to destroy someone.

These are some of the symptoms by which one can easily recognize this disease: *Anger* is a hate symptom. I need not tell those of you who read the Bible that anger is a very grievous sin and that Jesus said that whosoever is angry with his brother shall be in danger of the judgment.

Criticism is a hate reaction. By criticism I mean pointing out the faults of others and condemning them. Jesus said, "Judge not."

Quarreling is a hate reaction. The Christian may ·be involved in a rather heated discussion, but it will not get far unless it is fed by the fuel of hate and insult.

Name-calling is born of hate. Jesus said that whoever calls his brother names shall be in danger of going to hell (Matt. 5:22).

Stubbornness is a hate reaction. People who love others try to please and cooperate. If any one of you will watch yourself, you will find that when your antagonism rises to the surface, you begin to become very individualistic and contrary — you may even brag about your individualism.

Snubbing and *pouting* are hate symptoms. I mention these

together because one is the reaction to one who may have power over you and the other is the reaction to one over whom you have power.

Withdrawing is a hate reaction. Have you ever noticed that some people, when they can't get love, turn to seclusion? They build fences around their little domain and put up "keep out" signs. In lieu of love, some resort to activity, making money, research, or something else to fill the void.

Finally, hate is expressed in *indifference*. A man says, "I attend to my business and let the other fellow attend to his." He does not know that he is displaying his deep-seated hate, for "love is meddlesome."

HATE IS A HUMAN PROBLEM

Now, as I discuss hate, I would remind you that I am not thinking about the Chinese or the Russians or the Cubans. Nor am I thinking of church members in their pews. There are no two persons who, if they are thrown together for long, will not express hatred. It is our major human problem. If any man were to tell me he does not hate, I should quickly say to him, "What do you call it, then?" If we were completely rid of hate, we would be perfect. The best thing that we can do is to know that love and hate dwell within us, and in one way or another we must reckon with them every day.

The great French scientist, Louis Pasteur, once said: "Two contrary laws seem to be wrestling with one another nowadays, the one a law of blood and death ever imagining new means of destruction; the other a law of peace, work, and health ever evolving new means of delivering man from the scourges which beset him." The only thing that is wrong with this statement is the word "nowadays." It has always been so. Though we need to be concerned about world conditions, we must learn to handle the problem of hate in our families, in our churches, in our schools, and within the confines of our own country.

It is hard for us to believe that all the rest of the world is peopled by individuals who feel just like we do about things. They have within them what Edgar Allen Poe called "the imp of the perverse." Or as Matthew Arnold wrote a hundred years ago, "The same heart beats in every human breast!" We will be a long way toward solving our problems when we begin to use our imaginations and say to ourselves, "Since other people are made of the same human clay as we are, we must learn how to meet hatred; we must develop a technique of overcoming evil with good."

Did it never occur to you that this is precisely what the Christian religion is about? Most religions go no further than to teach man fairness, chastity, honesty, self-control, justice — within certain limits and as a rule. In other words, most religions try to curb the destructive tendencies of the human heart, to keep people from bashing one another's heads in, either physically or verbally. But the way of Christ goes much beyond that; it urges men to go out into the highways and hedges and find the multitudes who are emotionally starved and feed them on love and good will.

How Love Is Expressed

How, then, does love operate? We have seen that hate tears apart, leaves deep wounds, lights great fires of cruelty and intolerance, excavates great gulfs across which people stare in blank indifference and blame. But not love! Love is the pleasure we experience in being close to people. Love is talkative, listening, seeking, giving, going, waiting, hoping, bearing, forgiving.

Let me illustrate: It is a hot dusty road that you are traveling, and suddenly you hear that sinister sound of a tire going down. You are in a great hurry to get to your destination; so in anger and frustration you get out and prepare to soil your hands, your clothes, and your disposition by changing tires. At this moment a farmer strolls up and asks, "Gotta flat tire?"

If you take these words literally, you must concede that the farmer is either a fool or a blind man. But the implication of these words is really quite different from their literal meaning. The farmer is saying: "Hello, I can see you are in trouble. I'm a stranger to you, but I might be your friend now that I have a chance to be if I had any assurance that my friendship would be welcomed. Are you approachable? Are you a decent fellow? Would you appreciate it if I helped you?" Now that is what the farmer was driving at.

When we stop to think about it, all of us know how to express love. Yet half of the atmosphere of the world is charged with hatred. Some churches remind me of a room filled with highly inflammable gas; all you have to do to get an explosion is to strike one word. It is hate that charges us with tension and sorrow and bitterness. Harry Emerson Fosdick says, "Hating people is like burning down your own house to get rid of a rat." Fires like that burn daily. A good case can be made for the close relation between hate and bad health and insanity, and love and good health and happiness. We must love or perish.

REAL CHRISTIAN LOVE

We come now to the very heart of our understanding of love. Nearly everyone thinks that he loves people; but the truth is, most of us do not know real Christian love. Jesus deals with that in Matthew 5, to which reference has already been made. He said, in substance, that the trouble with our love is that it is not love at all; it is a shrewd business deal: "I will love you if you will love me, or show appreciation, or in some way feed my ego."

Christian love is very different from that. It says: "I will love you as you are, without any promise of change on your

part or return of my love. I will love you because you need my
love and I need to give it." Such love is redemptive. It binds
us together, inspires us, makes us live, and furnishes us with
the world's only cure for hate and loneliness and fear.

We can check our love by that of God as revealed in Jesus
Christ. I can best describe God's love by using three well-
known expressions. First, God's love knows no fences — neither
race nor nationality nor social group. He "loved the world."
So should our love be to every man. Second, with God there
are no forgotten men. It has been said of a man that "he loved
everyone in general and hated everyone in particular." Charles
Lamb, when asked if he knew a certain person whom he had
ridiculed, replied: "Know him! Of course I don't know him. I
never could hate anyone I know." Love seeks out the forgotten
man and does not leave him on the other side of the road to
bleed to death through the wounds of bitterness. Third, love
knows no favorite sons except those who most need the food of
love. Jesus majored on those who needed him most.

Dr. Frank C. Laubach has made great progress in teaching
illiterate peoples of the world to read. Dr. Laubach says of his
method:

> If you sit down beside an illiterate as an equal, your heart
> overflowing with love for him . . . , if you never frown nor
> criticize but look pleased and surprised, and praise him for his
> progress, a thousand silver threads wind about his heart and
> yours. You are the first educated man that ever looked at him
> except to swindle him, and he will be so mystified by your un-
> usual kindness, that he is likely to stop and ask: "How do you
> expect to get paid for this? I have no money." The only ir-
> resistible gospel is love in action. . . . If we serve the illiterates
> and then tell them the gospel after we have won their hearts,
> they will believe in Christ because they believe in us.[5]

---

5 Frank C. Laubach, quoted in *The Bible Speaks,* by Francis Carr Stifler
(New York: Duell, Sloan & Pearce, 1946), pp. 124, 125.

Admit Your Hate

Two things should be said about victory over hate. First, admit your hatred. Every man has within him a censor which we usually call conscience. This makes us ashamed of our antagonism. As a child we said to our parents, "I hate you," but soon we came to deny that natural truth. Now in adulthood, as any trained counselor can tell you, it is extremely difficult for us to be honest about this emotion. So we feel hate and avow love. But the Bible says, "Confess therefore your sins one to another, and pray one for another, that ye may be healed" (James 5:16 asv).

To illustrate further: A businessman sat at his desk, confronted by another businessman whom he knew had dealt with him unwisely, if not unethically. Instead of being hypocritical about his anger, he very frankly said to the man: "Now you just go right on out. I don't want to see you now. You know that you have presumed on me, and I am in no mood to discuss the matter with you. Come back in a couple of hours and I will try to talk to you about it." The second man, knowing that he was at fault, went out. When he came back, the matter was satisfactorily settled, and both were happy. They were both Christians. It pays to be frank with yourself about your hate and at the same time not to give it too long a leash. Nothing does a person more harm psychologically than to deny the truth about himself. To admit to yourself the presence of hatred is to have it pushed half out the door.

Love Needs Divine Aid

Keep in mind that love will not go far in conquering hate unless it has divine aid. Jeremiah said, "Can the Ethiopian change his skin, or the leopard his spots? then may ye also do good, that are accustomed to do evil" (Jer. 13:23). Ezekiel promised that the time would come when God will "take the

stony heart out of their flesh, and give them a heart of flesh"
(Ezek. 11:19). Jesus once said, "Do men gather grapes of
thorns, or figs of thistles? Even so every good tree bringeth
forth good fruit; but a corrupt tree bringeth forth evil fruit"
(Matt. 7:16-17). Remember that he told Nicodemus, "Ye
must be born again" (John 3:7). And the Apostle John wrote,
"We know that we have passed from death unto life, because
we love the brethren. He that loveth not his brother abideth
in death. Whosoever hateth his brother is a murderer: and
ye know that no murderer hath eternal life abiding in him"
(1 John 3:14-15).

These words have tremendous implications. Do you see
them? They mean that at the heart of all our social problems
— of war, of race, of poverty, of student protest, of drug abuse,
of crime — is the problem of the human heart. Hate cannot be
defeated by will power but by the power of our Creator. Furthermore, if we would increase the preponderance of love over
hate in the world, we must increase the number of true Christians.

Is there hope for love to win in this struggle? Of course
there is! Hate is suicide; it can never win. Don't be discouraged
if hate seems to win. We are not directing this warfare; our
business is to enlist on the right side and throw all our strength
into the battle. Sure, we have a great deal of hate in the world.
We have fires, too, but water will still put out the fires. The
trouble is, no one has the water at the right place at the right
time. Let us resolve earnestly that "for me and my house" we
will grow in love and let love grow in us.

CHAPTER FOUR

Is It Wrong To Love Yourself?

How do you feel about yourself? I mean simply, what do you think about yourself? Are you any good? Do you amount to anything in this world? Does it matter what becomes of you? Are you worth giving serious consideration to? Is it of any importance whether you are your best in life, whether you are saved or lost? Honestly, what do you think of your personal worth?

It has taken me years to see that the questions I have just asked are of tremendous importance. There is such confusion of thinking on this subject of self-love. Some think, with Martin Luther, that "to love is the same as to hate oneself." To such people, to be a Christian is always to belittle self, to disparage self, to try to get rid of self. On the other hand, there are those who love themselves with an intensity bordering on the ridiculous. They must have their way in every argument, and the least slight slays them. They spend their lives in a dog-eat-dog type of selfishness that is always camouflaged as service.

THE BIBLE ON SELF-LOVE

Some will be surprised to know that the Bible gives some very definite help on this subject.

To begin with, what was Jesus' viewpoint? He endorsed the commandment: "Thou shalt love thy neighbour as thyself."

Why did Jesus not say that we should love our neighbor as a brother or as a friend? First, this love that He talked about is not the love of friendship or of natural affection; it is determined good will toward a person whether we like him or not. Then, in the second place, Jesus knew that only those who love themselves properly can ever give their love to other people. Every healthy, saved soul loves himself with a degree of wisdom and humility that enables him to love God and his fellowman.

I think Jesus meant exactly what He said when He commanded us to love our neighbors as ourselves. He also said, "Lay up for yourselves treasures in heaven," and He condemned those who are "not rich toward God." He asked the people of His day, "What shall it profit a man, if he shall gain the whole world, and lose *his own* soul?" Notice the words, "for yourselves" and "his own soul." Suppose a person declares that he wishes to be selfish and lay up earthly treasures for himself and not be rich toward God or save his own soul. Christ has but one word for such twisted, damaged, deceived souls: "Ye will not come to me that ye might have life."

Let us look further in the New Testament. What did Paul feel about self-love? In Romans 12:3 he said that a man should not "think of himself more highly than he ought to think; but to think soberly, according as God hath dealt to every man the measure of faith." He did not tell us to call ourselves "worms of the dust" or "lice" or "animals." I often wonder why those people who like to call themselves "worms" don't go off somewhere and crawl in a hole. This world was made for the "grace-crowned sons of God." So Paul urged us not to overrate ourselves. I am reminded of the words of the famous Chinese Laotzu, who lived 604 years before Christ. He said:

> At no time in the world will a man who is sane
> Over-reach himself,
> Over-spend himself,
> Over-rate himself.

How Highly Should Man Think of Himself?

How highly ought a man to think of himself? The answer is easy: as highly as the facts would warrant. While we are not animals, we are not gods. As the correct translation of Psalm 8:4-6 (ASV) says: "What is man, that thou are mindful of him? And the son of man, that thou visitest him? For thou hast made him but little lower than God, and crownest him with glory and honor. Thou makest him to have dominion over the works of thy hands; Thou hast put all things under his feet."

How dare a man sink down to the animal level and say, "I am just a two-legged animal without feathers." Or, you may say with Lord Byron, "All men are intrinsically rascals, and I am sorry that not being a dog, I can't bite them." You may act like an animal, and even at times wish you were, but God created you for better things; and try as you will, you can never be satisfied with being a "devils' nobody."

Paul said, in his exhortations to husbands and wives in Ephesians, "So ought men to love their wives as their own bodies. He that loveth his wife loveth himself." Notice how frankly Paul considered self-love of a sort as natural and reasonable. He even says that "no man ever yet hated his own flesh." This, no doubt, means that a person normally does not hate himself, which is true.

But there is another side to this picture. As far back as human history goes, men have condemned the person who is extremely selfish, who is his own god. There is an English proverb which says, "Self-love makes the eyes blind." Selfishness is one of the greatest curses of the modern churches and of our world. But it has always been so.

Remember Narcissus?

Many of you have heard the story of Narcissus of the ancient Greek religion. He was the son of the river god, Cephissus. This young man was the very embodiment of conceit and egotism. He possessed rare beauty but even rarer vanity. He shunned all the girls, for he was in love with himself. One of these fair maidens prayed that he might someday know what it is to love and to meet no return of affection. The avenging goddess heard and caused Narcissus to stoop over a river brink, and as he looked at his own image, he fell in love with it. He talked to it, tried to embrace it, languished for it, pined for it, and died without being satisfied.

This is a marvelous, and perhaps exaggerated, picture of people who seem to be in love with themselves. And here is another picture from more modern times. In an English churchyard this inscription appears on an old forgotten tomb:

> Here lies a miser who lived for self,
> Whose aim in life was to gather pelf;
> Where he has gone and how he fares,
> Nobody knows and nobody cares.

To put it mildly, all the world hates the individual who loves himself inordinately. We laugh at him, we ridicule him, we shame him, we caricature him, we fear him, and we despise him. Perhaps someday we will have religion enough to understand him.

The Bible treats this phase of self-love also. Paul describes the last days as "perilous times" when "men shall be lovers of their own selves" and then lists some of the worst qualities of which mankind is capable, including "lovers of pleasures more than lovers of God" (2 Tim. 3:1-7). And Jesus mocked at the egotist in the parable of the rich man, who said: "What shall *I* do, because *I* have no room where to bestow *my* fruits? And he said, This will *I* do: *I* will pull down *my* barns, and build greater: and there will *I* bestow all *my* fruits and *my* goods. And *I* will say to *my* soul, Soul, thou hast much goods laid up for many years; take thine ease, eat, drink, and be merry" (Luke 12:17-19). These eleven personal pronouns must have been abhorrent to the Son of man, who came "not to be ministered unto, but to minister."

Jesus said plainly that "whosoever shall seek to save his life shall lose it; and whosoever shall lose his life shall preserve it" (Luke 17:33). He said further, as a final condition of discipleship, "If any man will come after me, let him deny himself, and take up his cross daily, and follow me" (Luke 9:23).

LOVE BEGINS WITH SELF-RENUNCIATION

Are you thinking that these passages contradict those quoted in the beginning? Not at all! No person can do God's will unless he realizes that he is not a king and cannot afford to "play king" for one moment. He must renounce or deny this extreme independence that lies deep in every life. This is done in repentance. Because every person is basically narcissistic, because deep within every one of us, especially in the child, there is the desire for omnipotence, we dare not indulge ourselves. The fact is, we never love God or our fellow-man unless we are to some extent dissatisfied with ourselves. Love for others begins with a kind of self-renunciation. We must tear ourselves from the throne and put God and our neighbor in their rightful places. Crass selfishness is overcome by loving ourselves too much to be inordinately selfish. In this love for God, which is the first commandment, we overcome covetousness, vanity, bad temper, adultery, drunkenness, dishonesty, jealousy, and every other kind of sin. All of us have said at times, "I think too much of myself to stoop to such." Or, as Joseph said to Potiphar's wife, "How then can I do this great wickedness, and sin against God?"

Perhaps some of you are thinking a bit cynically by now that what I am saying is, we ought to love ourselves a little and hate ourselves a little. That is not quite right. We ought to love ourselves wisely and well but not more than our fellow-man nor nearly so much as we love God. The Bible talks of four kinds of love: God's love for us, our love for God, our love for our fellow-man, and our love for ourselves. All of these are related in an individual's day-by-day experiences. For example, I know a man who does not believe in God's love, but his love for his fellow-man is very deficient because he does not love himself. When a man does not love himself, he cannot love his fellow-man; and when he does not understand God's love, he does not know how to love himself.

Selfish People Hate Themselves

Here we come to the very heart of the subject. It is a fact that any of us can observe that people who hate themselves cannot love other people. Extremely selfish people, to state the matter differently, are always people who hate themselves. When we hate ourselves,. we try to develop a false self by becoming identified with power, money, pleasure, education, fine clothes, or fame. It is a kind of substitute self. The selfish person's thinking runs along this line: "I am what I possess," or "I am what I know," or "I am what I enjoy." He is divorced from himself like the seller of a commodity is from his product. If he were normal, he would say: "I am I, a worthwhile being, created in the image of God. The most important thing in my life is not my money, my power, or my learning, but my character. To *be* is my goal. To do or achieve is secondary." As Hegel once said, "Be a person, and respect others as persons."

As already stated, only those who love themselves wisely can love others. Erich Fromm put it this way: "If a person can love only others, he cannot love at all." This is one of the most important insights in life. Many people wonder what is wrong with them. They ask, "Why cannot I love and trust God like other people?" Or they say, "People don't seem to like me. What is wrong with me that I express so much hate?" I can tell you in a sentence. You hate yourself! And your every act is self-centered and selfish. You don't fool anyone. People know when you are selfish to the core. You never will over-come it by any other means than honesty. You must begin by examining what you really think of yourself. Unless you re-spect and love yourself, you can never love either God or man.

How the Self-Hater Acts

The type of person who hates himself is sensitive and domi-neering. He demands of other people that they feed his ego. He is so insecure that the least criticism is an intolerable blow. If you ever cross him in an argument and win, he will beat you down at every point from there to the judgment. When he talks he says, "I," "me," "mine." He is usually very righteous and sometimes appears to be religious. But don't be deceived by this seeming religion. His is the religion of the Elder Brother and the Pharisees. He does not know what real Christian love is. He will love only those who are images of himself, only those whom he admires, as he states it.

More often than not, this strong, selfish person is out to save the world. Cocksure and domineering, he is very often 100 percent for the status quo. He is a dictator who hates himself and hurts other people, always justifying it in the name of some cause. It may be democracy, communism, or the church. Such people are a real danger in our world.

Another type that is similar but not exactly the same is the egotist who is always being imposed upon and hurt by the world. He complains and grumbles and resents and is never very well. He tells you how humble he is and why he is being misunderstood. He usually retreats from society and licks his wounds in private. But do you know what is wrong with such people? They hate themselves and are projecting that hatred onto others. They attribute hostility and injustice to others be-cause they feel these emotions so strongly.

Such people often go forth to reform the world. They are like the society woman who wrote to a social worker requesting to help rescue some poor children in New York City. She spoke at length of her shortcomings and imperfections, but hoped that her zeal would make up for her lack. The social worker wrote this brief reply: "Dear Madam: Your truly magnificent shortcomings at present are too great. Nothing could prevent you from visiting them on victims of your humility. I advise that you love yourself more before you squander your love on others." You see what he meant? Every social worker knows parents who hate themselves and damn their children by assuming perfectionism. Parents who hate themselves most are the ones who ruin their children. They never give true love. They either pamper their offspring or are downright cruel to them. And too frequently their justification is found in their concept of religion.

Distorted Christianity

One of the saddest things about the kind of Christian teaching many people get is that they think Jesus taught that to love God is to hate self. Religion, to them, becomes a kind of masochism — a punishment for self. There is an old hymn that says, "I would be nothing, nothing, nothing; Thou art my all in all." That is not Christianity; it is nearer Buddhism.

I know of a pastor who used to say, "The best is good enough for me." Sure! That is it! The best is what Jesus came to bring. "I am come that they might have life, . . . more abundantly," Jesus said. I am convinced that one of the biggest reasons people do not become Christians is that they do not love themselves well enough to choose the best.

Look around you if you do not believe that people hate themselves. How many people do you know who are really trying to be their best? Why do some people drink, gamble, use drugs, beat each other down, and generally make quite an unhappy mess of life? Some of them know better. They feel that their way of life is inferior. If they are not Christians, they will tell you frankly that they ought to be and intend to become Christians before they die.

If you were to tell some of these well-intentioned people that they allow hell to remain inside them because they do not care enough for themselves, they would immediately leap to their own defense. But that is the way all self-haters do; they are particularly adept at self-defense. People who accept themselves can take injustice as Jesus did. Some people are such poor church members because they think that they do not matter. Some older people say that they are "not worth anything" now that they are old. Shame on them! What would you think of a man who would sell a real diamond for a dime? Or what would you think of a person who would run down his house or his business or his children? Why should we, then, always belittle ourselves?

God pity us when we don't love ourselves enough to value ourselves and to choose the best, the very best, for ourselves.

YOU ARE IMPORTANT

This attitude presents a very great danger for democracy. Too many people are pessimists about themselves and decide that they are of little consequence; so they don't vote, they don't set a good example as citizens, they don't think for themselves, they don't think — period! We joke about the fact that 5 percent of our people do the thinking for the other 95 percent. But that is tragic! What we need in this world today is more people who have some convictions—not adolescents who yell for their rights —but mature Christians who will speak the truth in love. A person must learn to do good *for himself* in order that he may fulfill God's purpose in his life.

Why do you suppose those who work successfully with alcoholics never appeal to them to stay sober for anyone's sake except for their own? That is the only motive that works. If you appeal to an alcoholic to stay sober for his wife's or his

mother's or his children's, or even for God's sake, he will sooner or later fail. But God ordained that every normal man
should have enough love for himself not to destroy himself,
neither by drink or some other form of suicide. Love yourself.
For heaven's sake, don't say that it does not matter if you destroy yourself.

Think seriously about the stewardship of yourselves. Why
bury 90 percent of yourself in the earth, unused and unrecog-
nized? Did you ever think of the fact that, of all the people in
the world, of all those who have lived and of those who now
live, and even of those who will live, there never has been or
never will be another one just like you? God has made you for
your particular place in the world. Yet many people go
through life trying to be like other people. Born an original,
they die a copy. "Aunt Het," a comic cartoon character, once
expressed it this way: "Most folks are born to be like they are,
and every one is a good specimen of the kind he is. Salt is
awful if you expected it to be sugar, but it's just right if you're
thinking of salt. I'd be awful, too, if folks expected me to be
Garbo, but I'm a perfect example of me." This reminds me of
the words of the character Noah in the famous play, *Green
Pastures:* "I ain't very much, but I'se all I got." We never become divorced from ourselves, so why not try to become what
God intended us to be.

The Solution Is Love

You may wonder what this acceptance of our own individuality has to do with love. That is precisely what love is. To
love is to accept warmly every other person as he is, even God.
If we accept God as He is, we will worship and serve Him. If
we accept our neighbors, we will share with them. If we accept ourselves as we are, we will develop ourselves for the
kingdom of God. But we can never really overlook this unit
of sacred content called self. If we do not treat ourselves

right, we will certainly mistreat others. Shakespeare had it right: "Self-love, my liege, is not so vile a sin as self-neglecting."

Yes, we have a duty to self, for we are a part of our moral realm. We are one of our neighbors, so why mistreat ourselves? I might phrase the Golden Rule in the following manner: "Do unto yourself as you try to do to others." Or the commandment to love may be stated, "You shall love yourself as you love your neighbors."

Perhaps many of your questions about love, and especially self-love, can be answered by pointing you to God's love. All love is based on divine love. God made us to be capable of love. He loves each one of us. What, then, do we mean by love? Love is the respect, recognition, consideration, and care for other persons. That is the kind of love which God has for us. He loves us as we are. Do you see what that means? We are sinners, imperfect, small, and selfish, but God in Christ has become our Friend. He sees our limitations and our deformities, yet He is not satisfied with us. Love, then, says, "I love you because you are you and as you are. Will you permit me to help you?"

No doubt some are asking: "What can I do about the self-criticism, self-degradation, self-neglecting, and self-destruction which I have been heaping upon myself, and the hate I have consequently poured upon others? How can I get self off my hands? I want to love God and my neighbor, and even myself, as I ought."

The answer may be found in some famous words from the late General Booth, of the Salvation Army. He said, "Damnation comes from mirrors; salvation from windows." There you have it. Use your windows. Nature is a window through which you can study individuality; consider the leaves and the snowflakes, each one differing from every other one. Men are windows through whom you can see how you are made, for "the same heart beats in every human breast." But, more than these, the revelation of God is a window through which you can see yourself and God and your fellow-man in their proper proportions. Do you read the Bible? If you do not, no wonder you are wrong inside! Do you walk and talk with Jesus? If you do not, no wonder you do not value yourself! Jesus alone can save men from self-hatred.

Henry van Dyke once visited Alfred, Lord Tennyson, and when they parted the English poet laureate gave the great American poet a portrait of himself. Dr. van Dyke asked Lord Tennyson if he would inscribe on his portrait those lines from his poems which he would wish to be remembered though all the rest were forgotten. And Lord Tennyson, without hesitation, wrote on his portrait those memorable lines from "Locksley Hall":

> Love took up the harp of Life, and smote
> on all the chords with might;
> Smote the chord of Self, that, trembling,
> passed in music out of sight.

CHAPTER FIVE

On Loving People You Don't Like

Love your enemies." That is a very hard saying, as Jesus meant it. How in the world can Jesus expect us to love the Communists, the crooked politicians, or the money-mad businessmen — or, for that matter, those personal acquaintances who have said catty or cruel things about us!

All of us have enemies, actual or potential. We have people we do not like. They may not have done any particular thing against us. They may not even know that we do not like them. We do not want to kill them, but we do not want to have any dealings with them. Are we commanded to love such people?

The very idea of *commanding* us to love makes us wonder if Jesus did not have a special kind of experience in mind. Love as we usually think of it cannot be commanded. Would we command a mother to love her child? Either she feels normally tender and affectionate toward her child or she does not. Would we command a young man to love a particular young woman? The idea is laughable. Human love — romantic, friendly, parental — cannot be effected by effort.

What We Mean by Love

Let us examine this word "love." There are five Greek words which are often translated into English as "love." One of them is the word from which comes "erotic." Except in the

69

writings of Plato, it is usually used to denote self-seeking, instinctual, man-woman love; it is not used in the New Testament at all. Nor is another — a word for family affection.
But twenty-five times the word that is nearer to our word
"friendship" is used. Jesus often used it. It means to wish well,
to admire, or to be kindly disposed toward another.

The great word for love, appearing about one hundred
and fifty times in the New Testament, describes God's love
for the world, our love for God, love for neighbors and enemies, and even self-love. It is different from romantic love,
mother love, friendship, and even family love. It expresses
some of the most profound teachings of God's Word. If we
understand it, we will probably find a peace and joy that conditional love can never give.

Let us try, then, to discover the meaning of this mature,
divine, Christian love. Emil Brunner wrote of love as the "un-
conditional will to community"; it "has no limits and makes
no conditions." Shelley, the poet, called love "the universal
thirst for a communion not merely of the senses, but of our
whole nature." Paul Johnson defined this love as "growing
interest in, appreciation of, and responsibility for every person." Paul Tillich says that "love is the divine drive towards
the unity of the separated. Reunion presupposes separation
of that which belongs essentially together." According to his
view, God and man, and man and man belong together.

Love, then, is the *warm* acceptance of another person as
he is. It is not enough to practice, in Weatherand's words,
"a sustained determination to show unbreakable good will."
There must be warmth. Love is never cold. It also means a
full acceptance of another person. Anderson Scott speaks of
this as "recognition, consideration, care." Christian love always moves toward another without any intent of possession,
or reform, or domination — or even of dependence, for that
matter. Love cannot be passive, indifferent, or neutral, for
neutrality is a vicious sort of hatred. It surely is not passive

good nature. To say "I will leave him alone if he will leave me alone" or "He can go his way and I will go mine" is hatred, pure and simple. Love seeks fellowship, desires community, moves actively toward other persons.

An important factor in this definition of love is the phrase: *as he is*. To show love, the Christian must affirm the other's individuality. He must accept him as a whole, warmly, just as he is. That is what our world needs!

You see now why Ibsen, the Norwegian playwright, once said, "No word is so full of lies and traps as the little word 'love.'" And Rufus Jones in one of his last books remarked that love "is a word that needs a cleansing bath." What many people call love is either something indifferent, coldly passive, domineering, or unstable. Nor is real love spontaneous; if it were, we would have to wait for it to spring like a natural fountain. This love is the kind for which we are individually responsible; we can and we should command ourselves about it.

Now think how this applies to the people we do not like. All of us have trouble at this point. We like some people less than others, and at times our dislikes get very much out of hand. Even amiable Will Rogers, who is often quoted as never meeting a man he disliked, actually said, "I hardly ever met a man I didn't like."

Our enemies are not Russia or China, nor even the rioters in our own country. The people who really get in our hair are our in-laws, our competitors, our business associates, our club members, and even some church members. Let us ask ourselves, then, why some people are so hard to like. We may be able to admit that the trouble is within our own minds and hearts.

WHY WE HATE

Some people represent an attack on our values. As we grow up, we normally become identified with certain standards and ways of life. It is as if we swallow the ideals of our parents and those we admire. Then we think of ourselves in terms of this ideal self. In time, some people come along who attack this self. They criticize us, or they simply do not respect and admire us. They drink, they lie, they violate sex standards, or they live a pagan life — and our way of life is threatened by their pattern of conduct.

Some people directly hurt us. I know a man who will never go back to church because some church people gossiped about him. Another is "mad" at all lawyers because one double-crossed him. The injury may be social, economic, intellectual, religious, or personal; but it is always taken, consciously or unconsciously, as a personal injury. People do sometimes hurt us. Unfortunately, that is the kind of world we are living in.

Other people make us feel guilty. When they make us feel guilty, we are pricked in our conscience and then dislike them for bringing on the pain. Why do you think Jesus was crucified? One of the reasons certainly was that His very presence, as well as His teachings, made the Jewish leaders feel guilty. Men offer the cross or the hemlock to those who condemn them, even if the condemnation comes silently by the very goodness in another's life. We do not like people who are better than we are. Every parent and every pastor knows how guilt arouses hostility. Yet it is absolutely impossible to teach and preach the truth and at the same time keep people entirely comfortable.

We hate people whom we have hurt. This is a peculiar human trait, but it is a very common one. The Germans simply mistreated the Jews at first; then their hatred for them greatly increased. I have seen the same thing happen in homes. A husband may hurt his wife by unfaithfulness and soon become extremely cruel to her, as if he were punishing her for his fault. C. S. Lewis says, "The more cruel you are, the more you will hate; and the more you hate the more cruel you will become — and so, on and on, in a vicious circle for ever."[1]

Often we dislike people because we fear them. Children growing up in homes teetering on the brink of divorce usually hate their parents. We fear the Communists — and rightly so — therefore, we hate them. Catholics and Protestants fear each other; each blocks the other's program and are diametrically opposed on many issues. No amount of sentiment can avoid that painful fact. Real love might teach us to live in peace. But whoever creates a sense of insecurity in another will arouse his dislike.

Finally, much of our dislike is due to social labels. Our fathers hated the "Niggers" or the "Jews" or "labor," and we must guard against reacting in the same shameful stereotyped way. Jesus warned against name calling or labels (cf. Matt. 5:22). He knew the unfairness of social labels and the tendency to allow our prejudices to make for us a set of obsolete responses. Peter learned this lesson in the house of Cornelius: "God hath showed me that I should not call any man common or unclean" (Acts 10:28).

We need to remind ourselves that much is at stake in our attitudes. People judge Christ by the kind of Christians He produces. They turn away from us if we do not really love. Even our own spiritual health is involved. Unless we forgive others — for what they are as well as for what they have done — our own prayers will not be answered.

Do not be misled; hate runs deep in human life. Everyone expresses it, either in honesty or dishonesty, consciously or unconsciously. Sometimes we get sick because we are hostile and wish to make others wait on us. More often we get cold and distant toward others, and our way of life becomes formal and stereotyped.

A friend of mine has devised a simple quiz to test people's

---

1 C. S. Lewis, *Christian Behaviour* (New York: The Macmillan Company, 1952), pp. 51, 52.

honesty. He asks three questions. (1) Do you like most of the people most of the time? If they answer yes, he says that they are much like other people and may expect to get along without serious difficulty. (2) Do you dislike most of the people most of the time? If they say yes, he advises them to do something about their problem. Something is wrong, and they may have a crack-up if these attitudes continue. (3) Do you like all of the people all of the time? If they say yes to this, he says that they are just plain liars and there is no need for further questioning.

Although these questions are not profound, they highlight one of man's greatest problems — that of maintaining a wholesome attitude toward his fellow-man. Life is insecure. The human being is often inhuman. Simply to act like "all of the world is lovely and I am lovely too" does not square with the facts.

To test the depth of human hate, one needs only to watch and listen to a little child. When he is thwarted, he hates deeply although briefly. The dragon of revenge lurks in his dark mind. Hostility is volatile.

A little boy was locked in the clothes closet as punishment for his bad conduct. His mother thought that he must pay for his sin. But the boy did not quite see the justice involved. Later, when she noticed that the yelling and bad language had subsided, she tiptoed to the closed door and listened. All was quiet.

Finally, she said, "Johnny, what are you doing in there?"

No response. She opened the door quietly and repeated, "What are you doing?"

With tearful eyes and red face, he blurted out: "I spit on your coat, I spit on your dresses, I spit on your hat, I spit on your shoes, and I'm jes' sittin' here waitin' for more spit."

It is not easy to tolerate hate in any form. Even in its milder forms, such as neglect and indifference, it sometimes eats like an acid to the bone.

OVERCOME EVIL WITH GOOD

Let us look now at the divine method of meeting this destructive emotion. Many people have oversimplified the problem; they say that all we need to do is to understand the motivation of the offender. This may stanch the flow of revenge, but it is not love. Love is more than a kind of natural sympathy. Others say that the solution is to control self and not allow revenge, but this never rebuilds relationships or heals old wounds; this is not love either. Christian love is different from *anything* this world has ever produced.

When Confucius was asked about the rule to return good for evil, he said, "What then will return for good? No: return good for good; for evil, return justice." This sounds like a reasonable solution, but God pity us if we practice it. It will create wars and feuds and construct great gulfs across which men will glare in hate. Hate destroys, builds barriers, freezes out, and makes for unhappiness.

Jesus proclaimed a better method. It is unique, and we cannot say that it has failed because it has never been tried on any wide scale. It is not the passive resistance of Gandhi — really a questionable method of fighting back because it places all of the guilt on the other person and assumes his unreasonableness. It is not pacifism. It is not sulky cowardice which avoids all conflict.

Jesus' method is never to attempt personal revenge. We cannot trust ourselves to punish, even by the slightest coldness, those whom we do not like. Jesus himself did not. "When he was reviled, [he] reviled not again; when he suffered, he threatened not; but committed himself to him that judgeth righteously" (1 Peter 2:23). This does not mean that evil is not to be punished by law. One of the most Christian things, sometimes, a person can do is to prosecute the criminal. I have no patience with the kind of sissy, weak, "don't-do-anything-harsh" sort of behavior which passes for Christianity. Both softness and revenge are wrong.

Jesus' method is never to meet hostility with counterhostility. It is a sort of spiritual jujitsu. Take Jesus' words about going the second mile. A Roman soldier could compel a citizen to carry his baggage a mile. But what would happen if, instead of sullen anger, the citizen should say, "I'm going up the road another mile; would it help you if I carry this a little farther?" It would surprise him and perhaps change him.

Do good to them that hate you. Bless them and pray for them. The Negro spiritual has it: "You can talk about me just all you please, but I'll talk about you when I get on my knees." How can we ever break the deadlock of ill will against ill will and condemnation against condemnation unless we meet hate with love.

There is a remarkable story which came out of World War I about an Armenian nurse who had to tend a badly injured Turkish soldier. When she recognized him as the man who had killed her brother and had tried to kill her, too, she was severely tempted to neglect him and let him die. But she resolved, in the light of the teachings of Jesus, to do her duty. She nursed him back to health. All of us know human nature well enough to surmise the effects on the soldier.

Paul interpreted Jesus' teaching in these words: "Recompense to no man evil for evil. Provide things honest in the sight of all men. If it be possible, as much as lieth in you, live peaceably with all men. Dearly beloved, avenge not yourselves, but rather give place unto wrath: for it is written, Vengeance is mine; I will repay, saith the Lord. Therefore if thine enemy hunger, feed him; if he thirst, give him drink: for in so doing thou shalt heap coals of fire on his head. Be not overcome of evil, but overcome evil with good" (Rom. 12:17-21).

Try to build a relationship with all people, as far as our little lives may reach. If someone has misunderstood us and we might reconcile him by a personal visit, we are at liberty to modernize Jesus' counsel in Matthew 18:15-17, to get right up in the middle of the worship service and go to him. But we will act very foolishly if we try to turn these instructions into laws. Sometimes to go to an injured person would be a subtle kind of revenge. Many damaged souls would make only an adverse response to the overtures of a humble Christian. What Jesus is saying is that all of us are to work at this matter of fellowship, to seek community with all people, to earnestly desire a good relationship and try to achieve it. Peace among men is neither natural nor accidental; it is achieved by peace-*makers.*

OUTWITTED

He drew a circle that shut me out—
Heretic, rebel, a thing to flout.
But Love and I had the wit to win:
We drew a circle that took him in![2]

EDWIN MARKHAM

This kind of love is quite limited in the world. I have heard even church members say, "I don't care what so-and-so thinks of me." Well, I do! I seek the good will of all. Often I find myself cold or suspicious or critical of some other person. But it is not Christian. I desire warm acceptance from other people, and at my best I seek to give it to others — to all.

It is not surprising that someone has called the "love-your-enemies command" an "impossible imperative." Perhaps there is little complete forgiveness on the part of human beings. But this only emphasizes the fact that without God's help daily none of us can be Christian. To do God's will requires God's grace. With it we can discard our alibis and begin loving those people whom we do not naturally like. We have no right to reject our fellow human beings under any circumstances.

C. S. Lewis has said, "Don't waste time bothering whether

2 From *Masterpieces of Religious Verse,* ed. James D. Morrison (New York: Harper and Row, 1948), p. 402.

you 'love' your neighbor; act *as if you did*. As soon as we do this we find one of the great secrets. When you are behaving *as if* you loved someone, you will presently come to love him."[3] This is not the whole truth, as he points out (sometimes we love from wrong motives), but it is an important start in the right direction.

A traveler crossing the desert came at nightfall to a small tent where he sought food, rest, and shelter.

"What do you call your god?" asked the tent dweller.

"I do not believe in god," said the traveler. Thereupon, the man cast him out of the tent.

Later, the Lord appeared to the tent dweller in his troubled sleep and asked: "Where is your guest, my son?"

The man answered: "I put him out of the tent because he had no god."

Then the Lord said: "If you will go outside and look up, you will see by the light of the stars a sky far greater than the roof of your tent. I have not shut anyone out because he did not know as much as he ought to know. If I can give shelter to the unworthy in my vast world, could you not give your unworthy guest a little shelter in your tiny tent?"

"Love your enemies . . . that ye may be the children of your Father which is in heaven: for he maketh his sun to rise on the evil and on the good, and sendeth rain on the just and on the unjust" (Matt. 5:44-45). He tried to teach men that they were made to live in love and that only as they live united with God and man do they really live.

What Men Live By

Leo Tolstoy, the great Russian novelist, wrote a now-famous short story entitled, "What Men Live By."

Simon, a poverty-stricken shoemaker, set out from home

---

3 *Op. cit.*, pp. 52, 53.

with the family's small savings to buy a coat for his freezing wife. On the way, he passed a naked man hunched over on the steps of a chapel. In spite of his own need, Simon clothed the stranger as best he could and took him into his own home. Simon's wife, Matryona, was enraged because she still had no coat, and the stranger was only another mouth for her to feed. Her heart softened, however, so Michael became a member of the family. He learned the art of shoemaking rapidly, and his skill soon brought more business to the peasant home.

Although Simon and Matryona were kind to him, Michael never laughed or smiled — that is, he only smiled three times. He smiled once when the shoemaker and his wife had first shown their kindness to him, and again when an arrogant customer demanded that a pair of boots be made for him that would show no signs of wear for one year.

Strangely enough, the customer who had demanded such perfectly made boots died before he had reached his home after leaving the shoemaker.

One day, a well-dressed woman brought her little twin girls to be fitted for shoes. Michael could not keep his eyes from them. The woman explained that she had adopted the girls, left orphans when their mother died in childbirth. She had raised and loved them as if they were her own children. Suddenly, as she spoke, the room became bright where Michael was sitting, and he smiled again.

As soon as the woman had gone, Simon asked Michael to explain who he really was, why the room had become suddenly bright, and why he had only smiled on those three particular occasions.

This was his story:

He had been an angel in heaven. God had commanded him to go to earth for the soul of a woman who had just given birth to twins. Because the babies would surely die without her care, Michael returned to God without the soul of the mother. As punishment for his disobedience, God sent the angel back for the soul of the mother and then banished him from heaven until he could learn these three truths: *what there is in men; what is not given to men;* and *what men live by.*

He learned the first truth when Simon and Matryona took him in out of the cold: that in men there is love. He learned the second truth when he saw the angel of death standing at the shoulder of the arrogant customer: that men are not given to know what they will need for their bodies. He learned the third truth with the knowledge that a kind-hearted woman had adopted the orphaned babies: that men live not by the care of themselves but by love.

When the room had become bright in the corner where Michael was sitting, God had shown His complete forgiveness for his disobedience.

Before he returned to his real home in heaven, Michael said:

"I have learned that all men live not by care for themselves but by love.

"I remained alive when I was a man, not by care of myself but because love was present in a passer-by and because he and his wife pitied and loved me. The orphans remained alive, not because of their mother's care but because there was love in the heart of a woman, a stranger who pitied and cared for them. And all men live, not by the thought they spend on their own welfare but by the love for others that exists in them.

"I knew before that God gives life to men and that He wants them to live; now I understand more than that.

"I understand that God does not wish men to live apart, and, therefore, He does not reveal to them what each one needs for himself. He wishes them to live united; thus He reveals to each of them what is necessary for all.

"I have now understood that though it seems to men that they live by care for themselves, in truth, it is love alone by which they live. He who has love is in God, and God is in him, for God is love."

CHAPTER SIX

So You Want To Be Great

It was a cold, bitter winter in the White Hills of New England. A happy, humble family sat beside a warm fire chatting and jesting with the kind of contentment that comes only to good folk. The pitiless wind rattled the doors and wailed outside the windows. Suddenly footsteps sounded outside, and as the father opened the door, the whole family rose in friendly anticipation of a stranger who would come in out of the night.

It was a young man. His melancholy expression soon changed when he saw the warm, kindly reception of these simple people. He warmed his numb fingers and face before the fire and talked easily about his plans. He was on a long journey to Vermont.

As the stranger relaxed by the fire, a dull roar from the mountain above the house became a sound like heavy footsteps rushing down the steep side, taking such a leap in passing the cottage that it struck the precipice on the opposite side of the road. All in the family held their breath because they knew the sound.

"The old mountain has thrown a stone at us, for fear we should forget him," said the father, recovering himself. "He sometimes nods his head and threatens to come down; but we are old neighbors, and agree together pretty well upon the whole. Besides we have a sure place of refuge hard by if he should be coming in good earnest."

The young man, having finished his supper of bear's meat, began to reveal the secret of his character. He was obsessed with "a high and abstracted ambition." His cheeks glowed and his eyes flashed with enthusiasm as he unfolded his dream.

"As yet, I have done nothing. Were I to vanish from the earth to-morrow, none would know so much of me as you. . . . Not a soul would ask, 'Who was he? Whither did the wanderer go?' But I cannot die till I have achieved my destiny. Then, let Death come! I shall have built my monument!"

The family laughed a little at the frank ambition of the stranger; it was so foreign to their own. But the father admitted that he had been wishing that he owned a good farm in some other township and that he wanted to stand well with his neighbors and be called squire or sent to general court for a term or two. Then he would be satisfied with a slate gravestone with just his name and age and a verse of a hymn on it, something to let people know that he had "lived an honest man and died a Christian."

"There now!" cried the stranger; "it is our nature to desire a monument, be it slate or marble, or a pillar of granite, or a glorious memory in the universal heart of man."

Even the grandmother finally revealed her vanity. "Old folks have their notions as well as young ones," she said. She then requested that one of the family should hold a looking glass over her face as she lay in her coffin. "Who knows but I may take a glimpse at myself, and see whether all's right?"

"Old and young, we dream of graves and monuments," sighed the stranger, "I wonder how mariners feel when the ship is sinking, and they, unknown and undistinguished, are to be buried together in the ocean — that wide and nameless sepulchre?"

At that moment, there was a terrible roar and blast outside. The very foundations of the earth seemed to be shaken. Young and old shrieked in one breath, "The Slide! The Slide!" The whole group rushed out of the house to take refuge in what they deemed a safer spot. But it was too late; in unutterable horror, the whole family and the stranger were buried alive to be heard of no more.

Thus Hawthorne, in "The Ambitious Guest," tells the story of human longing and of the end of a dream of earthly immortality.

JESUS' VIEW OF GREATNESS

Of all people who ever walked this earth, Jesus knew that men and women everywhere want to be great. He is the world's greatest psychologist, to use a modern term. Tennyson called Him "the Greatest of the great"; and Carlyle spoke of Him as "the highest voice ever heard on this earth." He recognized that deep within everyone of us is the yen to be outstanding, to be distinguished, to be individuals who stand out from the mass. We all want to amount to something. The last thing we ever want to be said about us is that we are "nobody."

We can go further and say that not only does Jesus Christ know that we want to be great but He encourages us to want to be great. Listen to His words: "Whoever wants to be great among you must be your servant, and whoever wants to hold the first place among you must be your slave" (Matt. 20:26-27 Goodspeed).

"Whoever wants to be great." Think of these words. If most critical religious leaders were to complete that sentence, they would say, "Let him realize that his very desire is a sin and let him put it out of his mind." Modern secular thinkers would say, "Whoever wants to be great, let him assert himself; man can do anything he wants to do if he wants to bad enough."

The German philosopher, Nietzsche, was probably the most honest and outspoken critic of Christianity of the nineteenth century. He understood it — believe it or not — but re-

jected it in these words: Christianity is "the greatest of all
conceivable corruptions, the one immortal blemish on mankind." He cared only for the "superman" who must become
great by using the mass of men as dumb brutes, good only
for selfish ends.

But closer to home than the "superman" philosophy is the
spirit in our culture which places a premium on "keeping up
with the Joneses," becoming famous, and getting rich. Just a
few years ago, mothers dreamed of their sons becoming a minister of the gospel or president of the United States. Now they
are disappointed if he becomes a minister and pity him if he
becomes president. They would much prefer that he get to
Hollywood or be on a national television show. Too many parents consider themselves disgraced if their children are not
popular and well educated. We may be dishonest or vulgar or
immoral, but we must appear well in the eye of the public. It
is to be hoped that young people with such confused values
will experience a conversion *from* the ideals of their own
church-going, respectable, ambitious parents *to* Christ.

But what did Christ say about our desires to be great? Did
He condemn them as unworthy and ungodly? Not at all. He
made us that way. He had no use for the pale, sickly, cringing,
retreating, 'scuse-me-for-living attitude which some people call
Christian. These disciples of His who had spent three years
with Him did not come out with any self-effacing disposition.
He had inspired them not only to want to be somebody but to
want to be great.

James and John wanted to be great when they asked for
the chief places of honor in the Kingdom. Their mother said
to Jesus, "Give orders that these two sons of mine sit one at
your right and one at your left, when you are king" (Matt.
20:21 Goodspeed). And the other ten disciples were "pop-
ping mad" when they heard of their request; each of them had
hoped to be prime minister or secretary of state.

But what is wrong with such a request? Jesus explained

what was wrong: "You are trying to be great by the standards of the world. You are seeking honor from men and power over men. This is not God's way. The world's heroes are often heaven's villains, and vice versa. I will show you how to be great, and this will permanently satisfy these deep motives which I placed in every human breast."

Some of us Christians are going to face a serious reckoning at the judgment for the distortion of values which we have allowed by honoring selfish, unscrupulous men and women. If a man holds a certain position in our society, we blow our little pipes in the great unthinking parade of honor, whether the man was humble and Christian or bigoted and proud. Jesus said that His followers were to reverse the standards of the world, not encourage them. "It shall not be so among you."

WORLDLY GREATNESS

Think for a moment of the world's criteria of greatness: money, education, position, authority, popularity, pleasure. Dr. Blackwelder, a Lutheran pastor in Washington, D. C., tells of a young lady who said to him concerning a friend who is very talented in languages, "My, he's a great man. He can read eight languages."

The pastor replied, "Yes, he is a great fellow but not because he can speak eight languages for, you see, he could be a liar in all eight."

Even in the church more honor may be given to talent, to worldly success, and to education than to character, hard work, and humility. Some people don't care whether what the preacher says is the God's truth or not if he is interesting, entertaining, and "makes you feel good."

A young student accompanied Dr. Wallace Petty, a Baptist preacher, to hear Kagawa, the great Japanese Christian, when he was in this country. As they left the meeting, the student remarked on the "dismal" speech: not a fresh, vital, stimulating thing did Kagawa say. "Why," he said, "if he had not been Kagawa and you had not felt the obligation to courtesy, you would have walked out on him." But as they walked along, the student remembered something: "You know, as Kagawa was lecturing, I noticed those thick lenses covering his eyes. I remembered that he is going blind from trachoma. He got trachoma while helping the poor in the cities of his country. I could not forget that. I guess, Dr. Petty, when a man is hanging on a cross he doesn't *have* to say very much."

Recall for a moment Jesus' recipe for greatness. He said, in free translation, "If you want to be great, you must do the hard, dirty work of serving your fellow man. And if you want to be really great, outstandingly great, you must serve like a slave." We seem never to translate these words of Jesus into modern Christianity. If we get tired in the Master's service, instead of rejoicing that we can serve, we complain or pity ourselves. Instead of seeing how much work we can do in His church, many see how much they can avoid without feeling guilty.

The trouble with us is that it costs too much to be great; therefore, we hold on to our worldly standards and to mediocrity. It is easier because these pagan ideals are down in our bones. They were there before we were mature enough to become Christians. Some of us have seen in our history books the picture of King Canute being rowed down the River Dee by six tributary kings. Imagine the greatness of a king who could lord it over six other kings! Perhaps someday the history books will be rewritten, and we will be able to laugh at some of the puppet shows which man has put on. We might even learn to honor those who do not seek it and praise those who are surprised by it.

Our misguided vanity is so great that only the power of God can break its serpentine hold upon us. It is nearly impossible for us, when talking of some person, not to say, "He

makes a certain salary," or "He is the head of Blank Manu-
facturing Company," or "She has so many diamonds or has
traveled in such and such countries." When a friend told me
about a certain man who made a luxurious addition to his
house, I thought of the words of Cardinal Wolsey in Shakespeare's *King Henry VIII:*

> Farewell! a long farewell, to all my greatness!
> This is the state of man: to-day he puts forth
> The tender leaves of hopes; to-morrow blossoms,
> And bears his blushing honours thick upon him;
> The third day comes a frost, a killing frost,
> And, when he thinks, good easy man, full surely
> His greatness is a-ripening, nips his root,
> And then he falls, as I do.

STEPS TOWARD GREATNESS

But let us not think that because we see the superficiality
of our lives we will be able to mend our ways. The Christian
life is not that simple. We often *know* better than we *do;* so
I would like to suggest some definite steps toward greatness.

First, we must remember the tendency of our own nature
to be misled. We need to suspect our own hidden thoughts.
For example, Lady Astor at a large banquet made a convincing experiment: "It is a pity," she said, "that the most intelligent and learned men attach the least importance to their personal appearance. Why, right at this very table the most cul-
tured man is wearing the most clumsily knotted tie!" As if on
a given signal, every man in the room immediately put his
hand to his tie to straighten it. See what we really think of
ourselves!

Second, we need some new models. As long as we praise
public servants while privately admiring the selfish dema-
gogues, there is little chance for improvement. But our models,
the people we really hold in high esteem, are the ones who

mold our lives, sometimes unknown both to themselves and to us. It is almost as if we have swallowed the ideals of these people, and they become a part of our very emotions. This is why Jesus is so important to the true Christian. He is our model. We always know, whether we do it or not, that we should follow "in His steps." Albert Einstein said of Albert Schweitzer: "There, in this sorry world of ours, is a great man." And that suggests the kind of pull we feel to be like Jesus.

Finally, the only way to learn to serve is to serve. Shakespeare said, "Some are born great, some achieve greatness, and some have greatness thrust upon them." Don't you believe it! Any kind of greatness which is thrust upon you or to which you are born is not true greatness. The kind of greatness which Jesus had in mind is trudged out, ached out, worried out, prayed out — never handed out. To be a slave is to do things which others do not like to do. It means long hours, loss of pleasures, and usually criticism. It means self-sacrifice, but it is God's way. Jesus halts the whole human parade and puts it in reverse, with the last as the foremost. He puts the slaves, the scrubwomen, the cooks, and the "shoeshine" boys in the front, while the pompous and the proud bring up a tattered battalion at the rear. Lord, how our churches need to catch Your concept of greatness again!

Jesus' Greatness

I like the way Jesus summarized the meaning of His own life. It is a kind of spiritual and moral autobiography: "Just as the Son of Man has come not to be waited on, but to wait on other people, and to give his life to ransom many others" (Matt. 20:28 Goodspeed). So far in the history of the world the opposite to this has been the order of every day and area. The status of a person is judged by the number of people who serve him; if he is really great in the world's sight, he will never expect to do anything for himself. His attendants dress him, feed him, carry him, groom him. Jesus reversed all of this, notably in the upper room when He knelt and washed the feet of His disciples. And on another occasion He said, "I am among you as he that serveth" (Luke 22:27).

Are we to say, then, that Jesus became a great and famous man because He held to the ideal of service? I think not. He was great because He was God in the flesh and, as such, did the will of God perfectly. He served and made an issue of service as the way for a human being to live, because He wished to reveal man to man himself. His teaching was not like the modern slogan, "He profits most who serves best." Rather, His teachings are a call, a vocation. He said, "The servant is not greater than his Lord; as you have seen me wait on people, minister to them, so are you to make that the meaning of your life."

Over a hundred years ago Thomas Carlyle published a book called *Heroes and Hero Worship*. In it he said some very significant things about great men. "The history of what man has accomplished in this world is at bottom the history of the great men who have worked here." History is but "the biography of great men." His idea was that every great institution is the lengthened shadow of a great man.

Then he said in his essay, "The Hero as Divinity," that a "man's religion is the chief fact with regard to him." The Christian faith, like many others, aims specifically at producing great men. This does not mean simply that we aim at surrounding our heroes with worshipers. Many of the great Christians of the world are little, obscure people, like Mary of Bethany, Dorcas, and Titus.

For example, at Stanton Harold, near the heart of England, you will find an inscription on the wall of a chapel which tells of a man who sought to do something lasting during the days of the Cromwellian turmoil:

In the Year 1653
When All Things Sacred Were
Throughout the Nation
Either Demolished or Profaned
SIR ROBERT SHIRLEY BARONET
Founded This Church;
Whose Singular Praise It Is
To Have Done the Best Things
In the Worst Times
and
Hoped Them in the Most Calamitous.

Great men are like that. They have eyes to see little opportunities which are overlooked by those of us who are obsessed with our own importance. Great men do not start out to be great; they pile up such an accumulation of little deeds that they leave behind them a light that shines years after they have passed on.

William James was such a man. People crowded to hear him. Students patterned their writing and their thinking after his. He was a professor at Harvard University and one of the great philosophers and psychologists of his day.

One day a freshman was standing in front of a book store, looking in the window at a volume of O. Henry's stories. Mr. James came up and said to him, "Have you read the new one?"

"No," answered the freshman.

"Neither have I," said the professor, "but I have read all the others."

"He is great, though — don't you think so?" asked the freshman.

"Grand! Let's go in and buy this one." So they did.

Coming out of the store, Professor James said to the freshman, "You'd better come home to dinner with me; my folks are away, and I'm all alone tonight." He did not ask the freshman's name, and the young man took him for some instructor.

After dinner they lounged in easy chairs and talked — about football, about the big men among the students, about the things students liked and didn't like, about fraternities, college clubs, comic operas, and why one man was popular and another man was not. The freshman got the impression that the other man was about his own age.

Finally, at eleven o'clock the freshman started home. As he stood in the doorway telling Professor James what a good time he had had, the professor said to him, "You must come again, and we'll talk again." Then he added, "By the way, I don't think I know your name."

The freshman told him, and said, "And now may I ask yours?"

"William James," was his simple reply.

CHAPTER SEVEN

The Courage of Imperfection

Courage is armor
A blind man wears;
The calloused scar
Of outlived despairs:
Courage is Fear
That has said its prayers.[1]

These words suggest more than they proclaim. They show
us that we must live in uncertainty. Life can be dangerous as
well as beautiful. We become anxious. We get scared. We
fail. We despair. But we may also pray.

Dr. Paul Tillich defined courage as "the ethical act in
which man affirms his own being in spite of those elements of
his existence which conflict with his essential self-affirmation."
That sounds difficult, but it points to the fact that all of us are
looking at the world about us from within. What we see we
don't like. It doesn't make sense. It is contradictory and even
depressing. Who has not felt this sense of confusion?

And all the while, we are being looked at — by others and
by God. What they see does not look good either. When people look at the world and the people in it, they may cry out
with Emerson, "Everything God has made has a crack in it."
We might explain the crimes, the cruelties, the dictatorships,
and other bad behavior of man — although our explanations

1 Karle Wilson Baker, *Dreamers on Horseback* (Dallas: Southwest Press, 1931).

92

are usually superficial — but what will we say about the tornadoes, the floods, the hopeless idiots, the children born blind, and the earthquakes? These freaks of nature make us wonder. To define them as "acts of God" leaves us with a God who may be a monster.

The words "in spite of" become important. We have to act in spite of the seeming contradictions all about us. The world about us is dangerous in many ways. We do not have final answers to life's questions. We do suffer pain and disease in ways that do not make sense. Death does surround us like waters around an island. Man does wrong when he knows better. And in answer to the question, "If God be for us, who can be against us?" we may say truthfully and bitterly, "Man can!"

These are the hard facts that make us anxious. In 1348, from one-half to two-thirds of the people of England and Europe died from the Black Death. Anxiety is our "black death" — a disease which plagues all of us most of our lives and kills many of us. We may overcome many of our individual fears, such as the fear of the act of dying, but we all seem to have some measure of anxiety.

What Is Anxiety?

Rollo May illustrates anxiety this way. Suppose you are walking across a highway and see a car speeding toward you. Your heart beats faster as you focus your eyes on the distance between you and the car. You hurry across, and you feel some fear. But suppose as you hurry across the road you are surprised by other cars bearing down on you from the opposite direction. You are trapped. You are panicky. After the cars speed by, you are aware of a slight faintness and hollowness in the pit of the stomach. This is anxiety. We are threatened without knowing what steps to take.

Why are we anxious? Animals are not. We are "over-whelmed" when some value which we perceive as necessary to our existence is in danger. It may be our reputation, our fellowship with others, our self-respect, or our very existence. Man's concept of himself, of his self-esteem, is at the heart of his anxiety. Close to that is his awareness that he is partially free. Kierkegaard spoke of anxiety as "the dizziness of free-dom." But the foundation upon which all anxiety rests is our knowledge that we are limited, finite, human beings who are naturally insecure and must be often hurt and finally killed. We are anxious because we are insecure. That is why Tillich spoke of the "courage to accept our finiteness" as the best solu-tion to anxiety. We will see how this applies in a moment.

But, first, let us hear what the Bible has to say about courage.

The Bible on Courage

When Moses gave his farewell address to the people of Israel after thirty-eight terrible years of desert wanderings, he said, as they looked across Jordan at their enemies: "Be strong and of good courage, do not fear or be in dread of them: for it is the Lord your God who goes with you; he will not fail you or forsake you" (Deut. 31:6 RSV).

Joab, commander in chief of King David's army, faced a great host of Ammonites, Syrians, and some other hired sol-diers — forty or fifty thousand men. He said to the division commanders: "If the Syrians are too strong for me, then you shall help me; but if the Ammonites are too strong for you, then I will come and help you. Be of good courage, and let us play the man for our people, and for the cities of our God; and may the Lord do what seems good to him" (2 Sam. 10:11-12 RSV).

One of the choice passages is Psalm 27 (RSV), which be-gins, "The Lord is my light and my salvation; whom shall I fear? The Lord is the stronghold of my life; of whom shall I be afraid?" And it concludes with a great affirmation of personal faith: "I believe that I shall see the goodness of the Lord in the land of the living! Wait for the Lord; be strong, and let your heart take courage; yea, wait for the Lord!"

In the New Testament we find Jesus at Capernaum. Four men had brought to Him a paralytic lying upon a cot. When Jesus saw their faith, He said, "Take heart, my son; your sins are forgiven" (Matt. 9:2 RSV). The words "take heart" could have been translated, "have courage." He said, "Courage, my son." Can you imagine what these kind words meant to that discouraged person?

In the same chapter of Matthew (v. 22), He spoke to the woman who touched the fringe of His garment in desperate hope that she might be healed of a hemorrhage. Jesus turned and said, "Courage, daughter; your faith has made you well."

"Courage" was a favorite word with Jesus. When He came walking on the water to the disciples' boat, they were frightened almost out of their wits. "Courage, it is I; have no fear," were His words.

In the last, long conversation with His disciples before they were to see Him crucified, Jesus expressed the desire that they should have peace. "Peace I leave with you; my peace I give to you; not as the world gives do I give to you. Let not your hearts be troubled, neither let them be afraid" (John 14:27 RSV). But the peace would come through courage: "In the world you have tribulation; but be of good cheer, I have overcome the world" (John 16:33 RSV).

That word "tribulation" means pressed from all sides, as we say "hard pressed." And the "good cheer" is our word "courage." In other words: you will be hard pressed, but have courage, for I have overcome the world. He did not say, "I accept the world," or "I have made friends with the world," or "I renounce the world." He said, "I have overcome the world." He was encouraging them to follow Him in the same victory.

One more passage, this time from Paul, will be sufficient to show the Bible's view of courage. In the fifth chapter of his second letter to the Corinthians, the great apostle wrote of the anxiety we have as long as we are living on this earth (vv. 1-5). "For while we are still in this tent, we sigh with anxiety." But death means moving into another house. Ours is a tent here. The next one is of God's own making. "So we are always of good courage; we know that while we are at home in the body we are away from the Lord, for we walk by faith, not by sight. We are of good courage, and we would rather be away from the body and at home with the Lord. So whether we are at home or away, we make it our aim to please him" (5:6-9 RSV).

Now let us see how these Bible passages fit into workaday affairs.

DEATH AND SIN

Can anyone invade the solemn mystery of death? Poets and philosophers have tried to clothe it with wisdom and resignation. Doctors try — and thank God for their efforts — to make us comfortable as we come to die. Funeral parlors and florists do everything they can to make it look beautiful. Friends try to camouflage the stark fact by speaking of the dead as "having passed on." Ministers try to distract us by eulogies or passages on heaven.

But death, our own and others', remains a real threat to us. "Not to be" is rarely spoken of. Our transitoriness is seldom mentioned. Oh, we gloss over the fact of dying by saying that we would not want to live forever in such bodies in such a world. We rationalize that everyone has to die. We boast that we are not afraid to die. Some people even create childish superstitions of coming back to live on earth again.

But death, more than anything else in life, reminds us that we are human, that we are in the hands of God, that we are limited. And we go on dying with an uneasy conscience because somehow death is tied up in our thinking with punishment. In fact, it is the fact of death that makes us wonder about the real meaning of life. Death is the signature of life. Our bodies are so imperfect that we die whether we believe in death or not.

The pagan solution to our anxiety concerning death is a vague sort of immortality. The real alternative to Christianity is stoicism, modern or ancient. The Christian solution is bound up in Jesus Christ. When He becomes real to us, we admit our ignorance and face death by accepting the anxiety connected with it. Only Christ can give us the courage to say, "I die daily." At death the Christian finishes his work (on earth), but he does not finish his life.

Think, now, of our problem of sin. Sin is felt by us as guilt. It is true that some guilt feelings are neurotic and unreal. But all of us know ourselves to be limited, imperfect, wayward, wrong. Sin, in the Christian sense, means more than this, but this sense of sin is universal. We all know that we think and behave below our possibilities. We have all "sinned, and come short of the glory of God."

It is the anxiety that guilt produces that keeps us from doing even our best. We have failed, so what do we do to avoid facing our guilt? We adopt the current, local customs and try to avoid individual responsibility. We wear the cloak of conformity. Or we deny the concept of sin by declaring it negative; thus we join the cult of positive thinking. Or we admit that we are not as good as we ought to be but refuse to have anything to do with religion which allows a sense of guilt.

Still another approach is to affirm ourselves as sinners and try to forgive ourselves. But this is too easy a solution. What it really means is that we settle down in a sinful life and try to be satisfied with it. Or we may turn our problem over to some agency, like the church, just as we employ an investment company to invest our money, and thereby try to avoid anxiety. Usually such agencies make us pay something — like penances — which satisfies us to some extent.

But none of these is the Christian solution. The Christian not only accepts himself as a sinner but he judges himself. Rather, he accepts God's judgment in Christ. To excuse oneself, to forgive oneself, brings a kind of peace, but it does not bring growth.

When a man comes to Christ, he deals with himself in the light of the Cross. This means not only that he has been a sinner and is judged and forgiven, but he will continue to be a sinner and needs to hear Jesus' words, "Courage, thy sins are forgiven."

When Martin Luther told the timid Melancthon "to sin bravely," he was not trying to encourage him to do wrong. He was trying to deliver him from the puritanic effort to hold his sinning to a forgivable minimum. He knew that a man is not acceptable to God because he keeps the debit side of his ledger down to a reasonable minimum. Only repentance and the full acceptance of ourselves as sinners brings forgiveness.

I do not know why it is that God never allows us to completely overcome sin. Could it be because only in sin do we appreciate His grace? Paul said, "God has consigned all men to disobedience, that he may have mercy upon all" (Rom. 11:32 RSV).

The fact is, only as we have the courage to come to Him as sinners do we ever make any progress in overcoming our sinfulness. So we are utterly dependent upon Him for forgiveness for past sins and for grace in the present. If we cannot stand ourselves, we usually do one of two things: either repudiate ourselves or deceive ourselves. If we repudiate ourselves, we end in depression. If we deceive ourselves, we do not grow.

Pascal has said that "there are only two kinds of men: the righteous who believe themselves sinners; the rest, sinners,

who believe themselves righteous." This means that besides
the five ways I have mentioned of avoiding guilt feelings there
is really a sixth, hypocrisy.

The Pharisee who thanked God that he was better than
other men (Luke 18:11) is an example. He avoided the anxiety of guilt, of admitting his imperfection, by bragging on
himself and condemning others.

LIVING WITH PEOPLE

Let us discuss one other example of our permanent imperfections, *living with people*. It may seem a little odd to put
death and sin and living with people in the same class. I might
have mentioned search for truth, response to God, sickness,
catastrophe, work, and even sleep as being in this category.
All we do is imperfect and tends to discourage us. We must
accept the human situation in which God has placed us and
grow in it. We must not despair even in our failures.

Nothing is more disturbing, for example, than to experience physical illness, disease, and be feeling all of the time
that illness is out of place. In modern terms this is expressed
in the question, "Don't you think that if we had faith enough
we would be healed?" The answer to that is a firm, "Of course
not." We cannot boss God around by tricks of faith. Those
who have faith get sick and die like the rest of us. If God
chooses, He can heal us, surely. But He has chosen to allow
us to live in limited bodies and for a limited time.

In the same way, our human relations are always clouded
with imperfection. People misunderstand us. Our communication is inadequate. Some people withdraw from us and leave
us in loneliness — and what shock is worse for the human
spirit than a feeling of rejection! Good men get fired from
their jobs. Prejudiced people let us know that they do not like
us. Even friendships of long standing are broken.

What are we to think of these situations? Dare to go on

believing the best about men? Decide that we are at fault and try to change the situation? Deny that people are often hateful and rejecting, and declare that they mean well? None of these approaches worked with the Pharisees of Jesus' time. "He came to his own home, and his own people received him not" (John 1:11 RSV).

Here are some things that we are *not* to do. We are not to hate mankind. Hate is like burning down the barn to get rid of the rats. It never works. Nor can we afford to ignore other people. This is what Martin Buber means by treating man as an "it" instead of a "thou." "Hate is by nature blind," he says.

My wife's favorite joke is about the young man who was dancing with his best girl while another boy kept "breaking in." Finally he stopped, took off his glasses, and said to his girl, "Will you please hold my glasses?"

The girl became anxious and exclaimed, "Oh, you're not going to fight him, are you?"

"No, I just can't stand the sight of him."

We must not withdraw from people. Isolation is a form of hostility and may be born of fear.

A woman sitting in the ward of a mental hospital in a stupor would not talk, eat, or walk. Her facial expression was tense, her body rigid. She heard every word that was being said, but she cooperated with no one. I said to the psychiatrist in charge, "Is this woman angry or frightened?" His reply was, "Some of both. She is withdrawn within herself. We call this a catatonic stupor. She is schizoid. Someone must help her to come out of her shell. It is her reaction to anxiety. She must learn a better one."

I thought to myself, "This is one extreme; Jesus is the other." She fled from a harsh world, as she saw it. Jesus came *to* the same world. She avoided anxiety; he took it upon himself. She tried to save herself; he gave himself. She withheld; he yielded. This is the difference between sickness and health,

between hate and love. And in between these two extremes
loiters the whole of mankind.

THE COURAGEOUS APPROACH

What, then, is the courageous approach to people? Granted that approaching people will create anxiety as well as help
us to grow out of anxiety, how do we follow Christ in our
contacts?

It takes courage *not to judge* people. "Judge not, that you
be not judged. For with the judgment you pronounce you
will be judged, and the measure you give will be the measure
you get" (Matt. 7:1-2 RSV). "Who are you to pass judgment
on the servant of another? It is before his own master that he
stands or falls" (Rom. 14:4 RSV). "Leave it to the wrath of
God; for it is written, 'Vengeance is mine, I will repay, says
the Lord'" (Rom. 12:19 RSV).

Do you see what this means? It is the "courage of our
finiteness" again. We must decide to put ourselves in the place
of the offender, to become an offender with him. After all, the
biggest difference between people is that one person has one
set of sins, and the other another. We are all sinners together.
But it takes courage to accept this.

Then there is the act of love. "Love is the drive towards
the unity of the separated. Reunion supposes separation of
that which belongs essentially together." We belong in fellowship with one another, talking, serving, helping, living together. God tells us that. And deep within our hearts we know
that.

But this takes courage. We have to risk rejection. And
only those who are courageous, who will take the chances of
rebuff and misunderstanding and its consequent anxiety, will
try. There is anxiety connected with asking for friendship.
We have to be humble without being humiliated. We have to
act. Aggression and the freedom that goes with it may incur

failure. People are imperfect, and we must act in spite of the threat to our self-esteem.

This love that issues in the whole program of social action is at the heart of Christian living. There are few things that are wrong with the world that could not be changed if men and women were willing to suffer the anxiety connected with changing them. But instead, we tend to say "kismet" — it is fate. The modern form says, "It is just human nature and nothing can be done about it." Buber is right when he says that "the only thing that can become fate for a man is belief in fate." The Christian message says that God in Christ can change even human nature.

George Herbert Palmer, onetime professor of philosophy at Harvard, delivered a graduation address to a woman's college. It was entitled "The Glory of the Imperfect." The gist of it was, as I remember reading it, something like this: You girls are leaving a center of learning where there is music, art, beauty, and culture. You will return to communities where there is ugliness and crudity. What will you do? Become snobbish and arrogant and critical? Or will you accept these imperfections as a challenge? Creativity is the constructive approach. Yoy may change those conditions for the better only if you are willing to accept them first. It is a message for our day, especially for the Church.

The inevitable is that which we do not resist. But resisting involves anxiety, and anxiety must be taken upon ourselves with courage. And God gives us the courage as we relate ourselves to Him in prayer. That is why the poet, Karle Wilson Baker, is so right when she says that "courage is fear that has said its prayers."

CHAPTER EIGHT

Cultivating a Christian Conscience

The Apostle Paul stood before the Sanhedrin in Jerusalem and made an astounding statement: "Men and brethren, I have lived in all good conscience before God until this day" (Acts 23:1). Think of it! The man who said this had helped to stone Stephen! He had tried desperately to destroy Christianity!

The life of Paul ought to make all Christians a little suspicious of conscience. Maybe it is not so trustworthy as we have thought.

Most of us have heard someone say, "My conscience is clear." In fact, few of us ever show more human, indefensible pride than when we brag about having a good conscience. Such boasting is supposed to be bona fide evidence that we are morally pure and unblamable. But is it?

WE ALL HAVE CONSCIENCE

A man once remarked that his conscience was as good as new; it had never been used. Someone else said that he had never developed a conscience because he had considered it a liability; it never kept him from doing anything anyway; all it did was to keep him from enjoying sin.

But these remarks are in error. As Alan Richardson, modern English theologian, has said, "Every human being who is not clearly imbecile has a knowledge of right and wrong." And he could have said that every person suffers either consciously or unconsciously the "pangs of conscience." He does say, further, that all men "feel an obligation to do the right, even though they may perhaps hardly ever do it." In the second place, only diseased or distorted consciences are a liability, and I doubt that any one of us knows just when his conscience does or does not influence him. Then, finally, most people who brag that they do not use their consciences are really whistling to keep up their courage. They are probably suffering from a very keen conscience, and their method of shielding themselves against the anguish and pain of guilt is to deny completely its existence.

Few are the pains that hurt as bad as the pangs of conscience — that sinking feeling of shame and self-reproach that comes with the realization that your behavior has lost to you the affection and respect of some dear one. In the words of Huckleberry Finn, conscience is that part of a person that "takes up more room than all the rest of a person's insides."

Any normal person knows what is meant by "conscience" or "guilt feeling." It is the experience of knowing what one *ought* to do or what one *ought not* to do. This is common to all normal people, and to human beings alone. All that conscience says is that it is wrong to do wrong. *What* is wrong must be found out elsewhere. In other words, the capacity to feel a sense of guilt or failure is one of the things that sets human beings apart from animals.

New Conscience Develops

It may be well for us to ask how it happens that a person has a conscience on a given subject. Of course, the ability to make judgments, to evaluate, is innate. But what we say is good or bad depends on many analyzable factors.

Soon after a child is born, we begin to show him that certain ways of acting are approved and others are not approved. We punish him by words, frowns, or spankings, or we approve his action by smiles, pats, or other rewards. A child naturally wants to be accepted instead of rejected by his parents.

Even at one or two years of age his life is directed into certain channels by the approval or disapproval of his parents. As someone has said, "Conscience is what your mother told you before you were five." Actually, the approval or disapproval of other people is merely the stuff out of which conscience is made. It is the furniture of the conscience. The individual hears people say, "Shame on you," to himself or to others. He sees their look of rejection. Later, when he does wrong, something within him keeps whispering, "Shame on you! Shame on you!" At first he was spanked; now he spanks himself. And if a person has a good conscience, he may anticipate these "pangs" before the occasion of the misdeed and withstand the temptation.

Now the interesting and pathetic thing about conscience is that often a grown person never outgrows this immature conscience. What Mom and Dad said is still the last word. Things are still "naughty" just as their parents pronounced them. This is unfortunate because the taboos of childhood are not sufficient for maturity and because parents are often mistaken. Thus the "shelters of childhood become the prisons of maturity." Many people cannot do what they consciously know to be right because unconsciously they feel that it is wrong.

Any counselor could tell of hundreds of cases of unconscious, undeveloped consciences. A man may be depressed when he gets sick because he feels that he *ought* to be on the job. A woman may wear herself to a frazzle because every speck of dirt is not swallowed up by the vacuum cleaner. On the other hand, many of our consciences are overloaded with prohibitions (which was necessary in childhood) and yet be practically free from any warm, positive, constructive, Christian principles. The "thou shalt nots" frighten them to death, but the "thou shalts" leave them unmoved.

You Can't Trust Conscience

It is simply amazing how many people trust their consciences. If they feel a thing is right or wrong, it is just that way. Some believe that they have a faculty that is a kind of watchdog. When any evil comes around, they will hear the dog bark and know that it is wrong. Some think of conscience as a kind of information booth to which they can go and get the last word on any moral question. Others think of conscience as God's whip that is ordained of God to punish them for their sins. So as long as they "feel mean" about their sins, they feel good about themselves. They bargain with their consciences to let them do wrong, and they accept the punishment.

This is an unfortunate trick that the human mind plays on itself. People sow a big crop of wild oats, and then pray hard for a crop failure. But this is only their conscious prayer. Unconsciously they know that they must be punished. As Edmund Bergler points out: "Every criminal bargains inwardly for the electric chair: without this inner stipulation no criminal action is possible." This sounds strange, but it is probably correct. There is a certain element of self-destruction, as well as deception, in all sin. Religion needs to understand this better so that it might teach people to handle their consciences consciously.

Yet in a valuable book like *Peace of Mind* the author says, "We must learn to trust our consciences just as we learn to trust our eyes, nerves, and digestion." [1] This is a grave error.

Actually, a man may be entirely guilty before God when he feels that he is not guilty at all; or he may have a conscience

1 Joshua Liebman, *Peace of Mind* (New York: Simon and Schuster, Inc., 1946).

that gets all excited over trifles. Often, conscience is like a jammed car horn which blows long after it is needed. I have seen people punish themselves with deep depression over things which they could not possibly have avoided. And I have seen conscience pat people on the back who needed a sound spanking.

Paul did not have a conscience problem when he was destroying Christians. And the Pharisees in Jesus' time had quite a conscience over ceremonial handwashing but were bitter about providing for their parents (Mark 7:1-13). They paid tithes of little garden products but "omitted the weightier matters of the law, judgment, mercy, and faith."

The Egyptian mother felt no guilt in casting her child in the Nile; indeed, it was her conscience that so directed her. Infant murder has been practiced by many peoples with no sense of wrong, while no longer than three hundred years ago so-called witches were persecuted in our own land, and the judges and juries were obeying their consciences. There is a great deal of difference between the conscience of a Moscow factory worker, a Mohammedan with four wives, a Borneo head-hunter, and an American gangster. They all have in common consciences which are in some respects corrupted.

A comparison of two prominent men who lived in the eighteenth century will show how conscience is influenced by time and place: John Woolman and John Newton were contemporaries, and both were prominent religious leaders of their day. Woolman was the saintly Quaker whose inner light led him to protest so effectively against the slave trade as to awaken public opinion against it. Newton was the author of some of the finest hymns in the language. But he was also, for a time, the captain of a slaveship; and he has left it on record that some of his sweetest hours of divine communion were passed on this ship when he was separated by a few feet from a weltering cargo of kidnapped human beings whom he was transporting for sale like so many cattle. Newton's conscience could apparently take that in its stride; Woolman's conscience protested loudly. To represent both of these consciences as divine and infallible is not exactly convincing.

FOUR TYPES OF CONSCIENCES

Let us consider four types of conscience.

The *rationalized conscience* tries to explain away evil as merely "human opinion." All standards of right and wrong are relative. As Shakespeare said, "There is nothing either good or bad, but thinking makes it so." Such a person sits on his conscience and tries to keep it under lock and key. He is really an atheist who has no principle but expediency. His only fear is ostracism. His sins are secret sins, and he is kidding himself that he has solved his conscience problem. Has he? Not at all. Such people often have to drink to endure themselves. They don't feel close to people, and they are never free, vibrant, personalities.

People with a *childish conscience* believe that everything is still "naughty" that they were warned about when they were children. Their goals do not involve great social issues nor demand adult loyalties. Things are right or wrong because Mom or Dad said so. Their goals are often vague, and they are constantly frustrated by never accomplishing anything. Most of their ideals are negative, so they are always feeling guilty about something, and they can't help it. This may be illustrated by the homemaker who gets in a dither over every little mussed-up place in the room; or a businessman who can't take time to recover from an illness because of his childish conscience. He just has to meet certain less important standards, or he can't respect himself. Such people are filled with anxiety.

The man with the *superstitious conscience* is always punishing himself. He feels that God is a sort of tyrant who says,

"Now you have had so much fun, you must suffer so much punishment." Religion has often exploited this false sense of guilt by leading man to try to pay for his sins. But, worse than that, man often punishes himself by getting sick over his sins. Even some people work in the church as a payment for their forgiveness, but it is a poor moral experiment. The Pharisees were like that; they were legalists doing little things with a great deal of strictness in order to feel superior to other people.

The *Christian conscience* is very much better than the other types in that it is an ever-growing conscience. Bigger issues are seen. There is here an ever-expanding obligation to do the right that is not based on fear but love. A Christian must always reexamine his ideals. Conscience, to him, is the prompter. Standards and a way of life may change, ought to change, as he tries to follow his Lord. The Christian conscience is not overloaded with negatives; it involves positive morality — an adherence to the truth as revealed.

How to Develop a Christian Conscience

Some guidance needs to be given on developing a Christian conscience. It is so easy to assume that we are fixed, dated, and can do nothing about ourselves. On the other hand, many people are complacent when they ought to be concerned — asleep when they ought to be ashamed. Gladstone said, "The disease of an evil conscience is beyond the practice of all the physicians of all the countries in the world." That was true in Gladstone's day. But now reputable physicians have to deal with conscience. All except the wilfully ignorant know that many aches, pains, skin rashes, disturbances of appetite, and many other physical difficulties, are due to conscience problems. Dr. Leland E. Hinsie, the noted psychiatrist, says: "It is almost axiomatic that *people whose conscience does not bother them seldom succumb to psychosomatic or other types of neurotic troubles.*"

Religion, then, is interested in the whole man. God does not want man to break out with a rash; but neither does He want him to become so self-satisfied that he neglects to vote or to attend church. Consider, therefore, three aids in developing a Christian conscience.

First, check your standards by the Word of God and by human reason. The greatest problem the Christian has is how to know right from wrong. "There is no college for the conscience," said Theodore Parker. Paul said in his defense before Felix, "So I always take pains to have a clear conscience toward God and toward men" (Acts 24:16 RSV). He was saying, "I work at the business of keeping a clear conscience so far as duty to both God and man is concerned."

That is exactly what a Christian must do, work at keeping a clear conscience. It has to be kept up to date. No one can depend on the customs and ideals of the past generations, even of Christians, to guide conduct. He must search for injustices and failures with all the light of contemporary criticism and guide himself accordingly. For example, slavery was not generally considered a sin two hundred years ago, but almost all consciences condemn it today.

Second, the conscience must be cleansed by confession, repentance, and restitution. This is God's method. If we have wronged someone and can make it right, we should do so. Stolen money should be returned. Apologies should be made. But if no good could come of restitution, the Christian can only do one thing: he can confess his sins to God and expect forgiveness. The writer of Hebrews speaks of how the blood of Christ purges the conscience from dead works to serve the living God (9:11-14).

The Associated Press carried a report of a man in California who sent $3.00 to the Santa Fe Railroad station in Oklahoma City. He had stolen a ride in 1901, and did not want to face God with that dishonesty on his soul. The money was put in what the railroad company calls a "conscience fund." Others had sent in money for similar reasons.

Judas Iscariot brought back to the Jewish authorities his thirty pieces of silver. They said, "What is that to us? see thou to that." That is the hard, cold, ruthless way of the world. But Judas had only partly learned the message of the lowly Nazarene. He knew that restitution should be made, but he seemed not to have learned that God's love is such as gives a man a second chance. If he had understood the Cross, he would have known that love does not demand restitution; God takes our sins upon Himself and clears the conscience by forgiveness.

Third, to develop a Christian conscience, we must be thoroughly honest and sincere. When Jesus stooped down to write on the ground, in the presence of a condemned woman, the scribes and Pharisees sneaked away one by one, "being convicted by their own conscience" (John 8:9). He had said, "He that is without sin among you, let him first cast a stone at her." They were forced to be honest with themselves.

Paul wrote in his second letter to the Corinthian church: "Our rejoicing is this, the testimony of our conscience, that in simplicity and godly sincerity, not with fleshly wisdom, but by the grace of God, we have had our conversation in the world" (1:12). And to young Timothy he wrote: "Now the end of the commandment is charity out of a pure heart, and of a good conscience, and of faith unfeigned" (1 Tim. 1:5).

Rubber consciences that stretch to meet any opportunity to compromise are not Christian. Shakespeare spoke of "a conscience wide as hell." And Sterne, the eighteenth-century writer, said, "Trust that man in nothing who has not a conscience in everything." Perhaps the best expression of a true conscience is found in Coleridge's "Fears in Solitude":

> For never can true courage dwell with them,
> Who, playing tricks with conscience, dare not look
> At their own vices.

A ten-year-old girl was left, by the death of her mother, with five children to raise. The father, a day laborer, provided the best he could, but life became for the oldest daughter a continuing round of toil at the stove, the washboard, and the ironing board. All the neighbors praised her and admired her. But at seventeen she faced death from tuberculosis. A friend spoke to her with gentle reproof: "Why did you do it? You did not have to slave for these children. There would have been some way provided. They might have been put in an orphanage. You didn't have to do it." The answer was: "No, I guess I didn't have to. No one forced me to work as I did. But what about the *have to* inside me?"

This is the testimony of a heroine who had a true conscience. The *have to* within us may be healthy and helpful if we use it, educate it, and obey it.

CHAPTER NINE

Humility Is Still a Virtue

Phillips Brooks once said that when he began preaching, he wondered why everyone did not come to hear him, but after he had been preaching for a number of years he wondered why anyone came. If you have any humility it will probably be a good thing if you never find it out, for like the rest of the human race, you would probably be proud even of your humility. Humility which sees itself is not true humility; for as someone has said, "Humility is an eye which sees everything but itself."

Few people really want to be humble, at least in the sense in which most people think of humility. In fact, humility is in such bad repute, as popularly understood, that most of us would not want to admit being humble. It seems to be a weak, sissy, groveling, sniveling sort of virtue. We have all seen people who talked about their humility — like Uriah Heep in Dickens' novel — but had so many inconsistencies in their lives that we could not admire them.

HUMILITY MAY BE BAD

This kind of humility is a dangerous "virtue." It is the means by which people are often beaten down and kept down, by fear and shame. Religion has often resorted to this false kind of humility to keep people under control, make them obey. And it has done harm to human personality. It has become a "splendid vice."

Elton Trueblood has said, "True humility is not thinking badly of oneself, which is another form of attention to self; true humility is not thinking of oneself at all." This sounds good, but really it is an impossible ideal. We *must* think of ourselves. Our self-concept is essential to our self-direction.

The best way we can understand humility is to remember that a child, as he comes to realize that he is an individual, must first submit to his parents. The parents may control him by fear and shame. They may cause him to feel that if he does not squelch his own personality and accept the authority and power of others, he will be completely rejected. Such a child often comes to transfer to religion this kind of relationship he has had with his parents. In other words, if the parent did not allow him to be himself, he expects the same sort of injustice from God.

This kind of humility breeds authoritarianism. Authoritarianism means that we bow down to other people who may not be any better equipped than we are to think for themselves or to lead. We find it easier to become submissive than to stand upon our own feet and be the kind of human beings we were created to be. Authoritarianism in religion drives down pegs and says, "We now have the last word on the subject. Believe what we say and be saved! There is nothing more to be found out or to be revealed by God." Authoritarianism in culture is also a very vicious thing. It tends to label any deviation from past rules and customs as "bad." Authoritarianism in politics or economics, in which we assume that any present system is the best possible system, is equally bad. On every hand, in every realm of thought, we find people who prefer to remain in a static position rather than grow and reach out to greater approximation of the truth.

Thomas Huxley, the great scientist, in a letter to Charles

Kingsley, once said, "Science seems to me to teach in the highest and strongest manner, the great truth which is embodied in the Christian concept of entire surrender to the will of God. Sit down before the facts as a little child, be prepared to give up every preconceived notion, follow humbly wherever . . . nature leads you, or you shall learn nothing." This attitude of a true scientist is the attitude that people ought to have in religion or in any realm. It is the attitude of a little child. Jesus, no doubt, had this in mind when He said, "Except ye be converted, and become as little children, ye shall not enter into the kingdom of heaven."

HUMILITY DISTASTEFUL

But even true humility is distasteful to humanity.

To be humble, we must admit that there are limits to our knowledge. To grow we must be dissatisfied with ourselves. We must acknowledge our indebtedness. We must affirm that we are men and not gods.

Goethe pointed this out in a poem called "Limits of Humanity" (*"Grenzen der Menschheit"*):

> For against gods
> Let no man ever
> Measure himself.
> If he exalts himself
> And if he touches
> Stars with his head-top,
> Nowhere, then, can he find
> A secure footing,
> And clouds and wind
> Make easy sport of him.
>
> . . . .

What, then, distinguishes
Gods from all humans
That waves innumerable
Before them billow,
A stream eternal?
We are raised by the wave,
Overcome by the wave,
And sink beneath it.

There seems to be a deep desire on man's part to be a god. "Ye shall be as gods," said Satan to the first pair of human beings.

Paul Ramsey, a contemporary theologian, sees clearly that humility is not that "a great man [must] make a mistake about himself and think less highly of himself than he ought to think, or pretend to do so." On the other hand, he says, "There can be no true humility without some sense, implicit or explicit, of one's relation to God, an acknowledgment that man lives out his existence under a power and a goodness which are above him." He must depend on God "for everything he is and has."[1]

Perhaps "everything" is too strong a word. But man must depend upon God for the best things. He must not think for a moment that he is sufficient. God is God and man is man. As Karl Barth has pointed out: "The relation between such a God and such a man, and the relation between such a man and such a God, is for me the theme of the Bible and essence of philosophy."[2] Without this sense of inadequacy in the presence of God and without the hope that the revelation of God brings, man isolates himself from God. This is pride. It gives man a false sense of his "manness." He almost imagines himself to be a god. He plays God. He acts as if he were the "sufficient one."

---

1 Paul Ramsey, *Basic Christian Ethics* (New York: Charles Scribner's Sons, 1953).
2 *The Epistle to the Romans,* trans. Edwyn C. Hoskyns (6th edition. New York: Oxford University Press, 1933), p. 10.

He may declare that he cannot understand grace, or faith, or repentance, or justification. But the truth is that he resists God unconsciously, and consciously rationalizes against Him. Therefore, Christian humility is a religious doctrine. Therefore, also, it is a decision. He says yes to God and no to the ungodly inner demand to be a god.

This sounds strange, doesn't it? But it is true. And the Bible is trying to tell us over and over that humility is the mainspring of all other human virtues. "God resisteth the proud, but giveth grace unto the humble. . . . Humble yourselves in the sight of the Lord, and he shall lift you up" (James 4:6, 10).

HUMILITY IN THE NEW TESTAMENT

Throughout the Gospels we find Jesus emphasizing humility. His very life was an expression of it. Why was He born in a stable in an insignificant little town? Why was His earthly family chosen from ordinary people? Why from a little town in Nazareth? Why a life of plain hard work, carpentering in Nazareth, until He was thirty years of age? Why even in His public ministry, when many no doubt would have ministered unto Him and when He was performing miracles on every hand, did He choose to live in poverty and in lowliness? Why did He die upon a cross?

In Luke 14:7-11, we have some words from the Master in which He instructs His disciples not to take the highest room when they were bidden to a feast, but to choose a lowly place and then wait for the host to invite them to something better. He spoke these words in the house of Simon, the Pharisee, when He was there for sabbath dinner. It was not a lesson in table manners that He was primarily interested in, but a lesson in spiritual living. He saw these social climbers destroying their peace of mind and their social usefulness by the wrong idea of life.

Do you remember the picture that the Master gave of two people who went to church one day? One of them was a strictly righteous man. He stood up to pray in public, and he thanked God that he was better than other people. He did his religious duty and grew increasingly proud and deformed in the process. The other man, who knew himself to be a sinner and was willing to admit his deficiencies, prayed, "God be merciful to me a sinner." Jesus said this man went down to his house justified rather than the other. Then He repeated to this group of people what He often said, "Every one that exalteth himself shall be abased; and he that humbleth himself shall be exalted" (Luke 18:14).

Or do you remember the Master's putting a towel about His waist and, stooping down like a servant, washing the feet of His disciples in that upper room? They were astounded! Peter even refused at first to have his feet washed, but the Master said, "I am doing this as a lesson in humility; as I have stooped down to serve you, so you are to serve each other."

The Apostle Paul summarized the whole spirit of Christ when he wrote Philippians 2:5-11. The gist of what he said is this. Jesus did not resent giving up the form of God when He came to this earth, but He emptied himself even of His divine reputation and assumed the form of a slave. As a human being, He humbled Himself and became obedient unto death — even the death of the cross. Then Paul said two significant things about Christ. One is, "Wherefore God also hath highly exalted him." And earlier in this passage he said, "Let this mind be in you, which was also in Christ Jesus" — that of not demanding for ourselves, of not thinking that we should have to hold on to what we have, but rather of being willing to sacrifice in order to do the will of God.

Those early Christians, many of them, caught this spirit. They understood what the Master was talking about. For example, when Peter was entering the house of Cornelius, the Roman centurion "fell down at his feet, and worshiped him."

But Peter lifted him up and said, "Stand up; I myself also am a man." The Apostle Paul had the same approach at Lystra. The people wanted to worship him when they saw the miracles that he did. They said, "This man is Mercury," for he was the chief speaker; and Barnabas, who was with him, was thought to be Jupiter. The people were ready to offer sacrifices to them. But Paul and Barnabas tore their clothes and ran among the people, saying, "Sirs, why do ye these things? We also are men of like passions with you" (Acts 14:15).

You see, humility is a very practical doctrine. It is not putting ourselves down into the dust, even though the word itself comes from the Latin word for earth. It means that we are of the earth — earthy. It also means that we are come from God. While we are not worms of the dust, neither are we gods. Humility puts man in his place, but primarily it is a doctrine of relationship, a doctrine that says, "I must find my proper place in relationship to my fellow human beings and God." So let us think of some of the tests of humility.

HUMILITY AND FRUSTRATION

First, one of the best tests of whether a man is truly humble is how he reacts to frustration. How do you act when you are blocked on the road to some cherished goal? Not long ago, I was talking on the subject of humility, and a friend brought me a little plaque with this message:

> Humility is perpetual quietness of heart. It is to have no trouble. It is never to be fretted or vexed, irritable or sore; to wonder at nothing that is done to me, to feel nothing done against me. It is to be at rest when nobody praises me, and when I am blamed or despised, it is to have a blessed home in myself where I can go in and shut the door and kneel to my Father in secret and be at peace, as in a deep sea of calmness, when all around and about me is seeming trouble.

Many times when we are sick we cannot do the things we can normally do when we are well, and we react like children — we pity ourselves. We are overcome or overwhelmed by feelings of worthlessness. Or when we fail, we find ourselves saying, "We should not have failed." It is a blow to our self-regard. Or think of old age. It is a tragedy to a person who is proud. One hates to lose her beauty; another hates to lose his youth. Neither can stand the loss and be happy.

One feature that I enjoy in the *Saturday Review* is the section of advertisements in the back of it. One of them recently said, "Middle-aged woman, educated beyond endurance, wants fling in far-away places, preferably Asia." Think of it! I know some people who are "educated beyond endurance"— you can hardly endure *them*. Many people in the world feel exactly as that woman does. They do not know that life sometimes circumscribe them.

REACTION TO SUCCESS

In the second place, how do you take success or power? A man who is not humble, the minute he has power, will begin to "throw his weight around," to feel that he now has the right to exert influence over other people and, if necessary, to crush them. But a big man is one who puts himself down on the level of those who may not have the same standing as he has with the crowd.

Dr. Hofstadter, associate professor of history at Columbia University, wrote a book a few years ago in which he says this of Abraham Lincoln: "The best measure of Lincoln's personal eminence in the human calendar, is that he was chastened, and not intoxicated by power."

All of us have seen men who could not resist that temptation. A person gets a little education or makes some money, and immediately he gets more and more selfish, bigoted, narrow, and self-centered. But the truly great man is the one who realizes that he is a steward of that which God has given him

— that if he has been given talents to make money or to influence people, he has even greater responsibility in using these talents well before his Creator.

I remember, for example, reading a few years ago that Kagawa, the great Japanese Christian, was at that time drawing what would be in our money about $90,000 a year royalties on his writings. But he was living in a little five-room house, his wife and children with him, and no servants. He might easily have lived sumptuously before his fellows, but he proposed to live like he felt Christ had lived. Once he was offered a job as head of the welfare department in a large Japanese city, and he said, "I will not take the salary [which was $10,000 a year]; but if you want me to take the job without the salary, I shall be glad to do so."

GETTING ALONG WITH PEOPLE

Another test of your humility is how you get along with other people. Think of the elder brother of the so-called prodigal son when he found that his younger brother had gone away from home. He must have been very glad to get rid of him. At least when he returned, the elder brother "was mad and would not come in." Such a spirit often finds itself expressed in churches. People get mad and arrogant and intolerant toward each other. That spirit affects the business world, too. How do you feel about your competitors? How do you get along with them? Can you look at their faults with understanding? Do you envy them? Do you find yourself hating them?

Again, we must show humility toward those who may be less fortunate than we. Think of the masterful story that Christ told of the good Samaritan. The priest and the Levite were too busy with "big" things, as they thought of them, to take time to bind up the wounds of the man on the road. But the Samaritan was not too good to soil his hands or his clothes by taking care of this distressed person. A man who feels that he is better than other people is always a man who is little, unconscious that he needs the sympathy of people because he is a damaged soul. When you find a humble man, you find a man who does not think he is better than other human beings. He may realize that he has something that they do not have in some respects, but he knows also that God has made us as individuals to live and to act in our distinctive capacities.

Spinoza said, "Pride is the pleasure arising from a man's thinking too highly of himself." And Alexander Pope, the English poet, spoke of pride as the "never-failing vice of fools." Wordsworth described a man who "with the food of pride sustained his soul in solitude." Then he said,

> ... henceforth be warned, and know that pride,
> Howe'er disguised in its own majesty,
> Is littleness; that he who feels contempt
> For any living thing, hath faculties
> Which he has never used; that thought with him
> Is in its infancy.

I doubt that you could find a better description of the difference between humility and pride than these lines. When you find a man who thinks he is better than other men, you find a man who has not thought but rather has used labels as devices to keep himself from thinking.

Laotzu, who was born about 604 B.C., said:

> Standing tiptoe a man loses balance,
> Walking astride he has no pace,
> Kindling himself he fails to light,
> Acquitting himself he forfeits his hearers,
> Admiring himself he does so alone.
> Pride has never brought a man greatness
> But, according to the way of life,
> Brings the ills that make him unfit,
> Make him unclean in the eyes of his neighbor,
> And a sane man will have none of them.[3]

3 Witter Bynner, *The Way of Life According to Laotzu* (New York: The John Day Company, 1944), p. 39.

How do you get along with other people? When you are around them, do you put them at ease — can they know that you are not going to hurt them, that you respect them — or do you put yourself higher and wait for them to knock you off your pedestal? Proud people unconsciously invite attack by others even if they say nothing, but humble people are always in a position to serve others because they know that they are made of the same clay as all the rest of the human race.

HUMILITY AND RELIGION

A fourth test of humility is how a man reacts to the claims of the Christian faith. We often overlook the fact that religion is one of the best indexes to personality, to what really makes us "tick" inside. For example, salvation is a very odious word to people who are not humble. Who are we to need saving? Does a man have to have help from someone else? Can't he stand on his own feet and be self-reliant? That is the attitude of the world. Why should I need someone to save me? I'm getting along all right.

Or take prayer. Why should I pray? I can run my own life. I'm not under obligation to bow down and confess my sins to God. I do not owe anyone anything. I live my own life. I make my own way. Why should I be calling on some-one for help? That is the attitude of a man who is proud.

Or better still, look at our attitude toward obedience. We know that moral laws are right. But when a man is proud, he feels that he is an exception, that it is not his business to obey God. Even though it is good for the masses, it is not necessary that he humble himself and abide by the laws of God or man. So instead of being obedient, he either secretly, or sometimes publicly, defies the law and says, "As much as I can, I will do as I please."

No lowly service, no binding of the wounds of the beaten,

no washing of saints' feet, no confession of sins, no sacrifice — not for those people who have never learned humility.

Yet it seems such a foolish thing for us to think so well of ourselves and to put ourselves so high when, after all, we are poor, weak, distressed, needy human beings.

As we think of the brevity of life and the fact that we have but a few years to strut upon this stage, we remember,

> 'Tis the wink of an eye, 'tis the draught of a breath,
> From the blossom of health to the paleness of death,
> From the gilded saloon to the bier and the shroud —
> Oh, why should the spirit of mortal be proud?

One of the things that we have to remember, as we sit in church and think of our responsibilities before God, is that we are no exception to God's rule. When He calls and presents His will to man, every man must realize that this applies equally to him, that God is no respecter of persons.

Marquis James, in his biography of Andrew Jackson, tells a very interesting story about an incident that occurred in Nashville, Tennessee, in October, 1818. Peter Cartwright, the most famous of the pioneer circuit-rider preachers, was attending a Methodist conference in Nashville and was asked to preach at one of the churches on Sunday. Great crowds came to hear him. During the service, Jackson walked into the auditorium and, not being able to find a seat, walked down a little way from the back, leaned against a pillar, and stood there listening. When the pastor of the church saw that Andrew Jackson had come in, he leaned over and pulled the coattail of the preacher, Peter Cartwright, and whispered loud enough for half the congregation to hear, "General Jackson has come in." Rugged old Peter Cartwright was furious. He looked at the preacher a moment and then confronted the crowd with these words, "Who is General Jackson? If he does not get his soul converted, God will damn him as quick as a Guinea Nigger."

Some of the people said to Peter Cartwright at the close of the service, "General Jackson will chastise you for your insolence," to which this frontier preacher said, "Two can play at that game." Instead, he accepted an invitation to preach that afternoon at a little country church close to the Hermitage, General Jackson's home. General Jackson admired a man who thought for himself and stood for something, and so he invited Peter Cartwright home with him that day for dinner! He was a man's man! One who knew that all men stood equally before God.

God calls us today to a new kind of humility. The humility of Jesus Christ, who held up His head and stood as the Son of God, proclaimed the word of God and the will of God and bowed down to no man. At the same time, He did bow, from the very first of His earthly life until the last the disciples saw of Him, before His Father. Always He was seeking the will of the Father. That is the kind of humility we need today. It is the kind of humility to which God calls us, which will straighten us out in our relationships with each other, and will cause us to enjoy the relationships with our fellow-man and with our Heavenly Father.

CHAPTER TEN

Learning To Manage Myself

I am my world's number one problem. All of the "problems" of mankind have arisen because people like myself could not manage themselves. Of course, it would be more flattering to me if I could say that the problem people of the world are not in my class; they are across the tracks or out in the country or members of another religious faith. But such is not the case. Even if I had managed myself well up to this present moment — which I haven't — there is nothing to keep me from becoming a failure an hour from now.

The Bible puts this matter plainly. "So the man who thinks he stands securely must be on the lookout not to fall" (1 Cor. 10:12 Williams). "Brothers, if anybody is caught in the very act of doing wrong, you who are spiritual, in the spirit of gentleness, must set him right; each of you continuing to think of yourself, for you may be tempted too" (Gal. 6:1 Williams). Or the words of the Master himself ought to stab us wide awake: "You must all keep watching and praying that you may not be exposed to temptation. Man's spirit is willing but human nature is weak" (Matt. 26:41 Williams).

One of the most remarkable aspects of the Bible is its honest facing of human failure and weakness.

I Am My Problem

Somewhere there is a line of poetry which says, "When the

rose decks herself, she adorns the garden!" My obligation to be an attractive, stable, worthwhile Christian is certainly a primary one. I may work hard in the church or in the community; I may provide well for my family; I may produce so far as service is concerned — but if I am not the kind of person who is a good example of my religion, I am missing my greatest opportunity. Is that not the meaning of 1 Corinthians 13?

It is simpler in the case of the rose. It grows automatically, so far as we human beings know. In our case, life will not stand still. We never step into the same stream twice, as the ancients put it. Life changes. We change. Even after we get right we have the problem of staying right. Today, I may be comparatively poised, happy, and useful. Tomorrow, I may be overwhelmed by tragedy, may be whimpering and dejected. There are mood swings within and weather conditions, wars, and economic depressions without. There is tremendous social pressure, conscious and unconscious, that envelops us on the one hand; there are wild, irrational, biological and egocentric drives which arise from within, on the other.

Sometimes we hanker for a social group which will control us (although we never quite put it in these words); some stable, non-threatening, directing institution or social setting where we will not have so many conflicts and so many decisions to make. Instead our world is in a state of flux. Rural and town young people go away to college and to war. City people, young and old, are living next door to people they do not know or, if they do, they do not like. On religion, social customs, morals and education we do not agree, and we do not feel close to one another. We need more of a sense of belonging, but, at present and in the near future, it is very unlikely that we can depend on that personal support.

Dr. Lewis J. Sherrill of Union Seminary in New York has put it this way: "Modern civilization requires that the individual be a person of extraordinary strength if he is to thrive in the midst of that civilization . . . And yet, on the other hand, modern society is producing, in vast numbers, persons who are rendered deficient because they cannot achieve precisely that kind of strength and maturity which our civilization demands."[1]

PAUL'S VIEW

The Apostle Paul faces the problem of self-management, even after years of Christian work: "Any man who enters an athletic contest practices rigid self-control in training, only to win a wreath that withers, but we are in to win a wreath that never withers. So that is the way I run, with no uncertainty as to winning. That is the way I box, not like one that punches the air. But I keep on beating and bruising my body and making it my slave, so that I, after I have summoned others to the race, may not myself become unfit to run" (1 Cor. 9:25-27 Williams).

This vivid and bold figure is taken from the great athletic festivals of the day. To excel — to win the cup, in modern parlance — was the height of ambition for man. Paul's goal was Christlike character and the reward of a life spent for Christ. So he declares the strenuousness of this character-task. (See also Rom. 8:13; 1 Cor. 4:11f.; 2 Cor. 4:7f.; Col. 3:5; 1 Peter 4:1.) Like athletic exercises, it requires discipline. Paul was a spiritual pugilist, as every Christian worth the name must be.

He was not interested in shadow-boxing. That is the practice of those who are unskilled in the ring and, in religious life, corresponds to the self-punishing fasts and self-denials that are prescribed. Many people waste good energy trying to get themselves in shape to live the Christian life. They are told that fasting will serve as an antidote for fast living. At Easter

---

1 Lewis J. Sherrill, *The Struggle of the Soul* (New York: The Macmillan Company, 1952), p. 1.

they leave off tobacco or alcoholic beverages or certain foods. It seems never to occur to them to question, "Is there a carry-over? Is there, to put it in modern language, any transfer of training?" Some of us have experimented with fasting and found it wanting. No "beating the air" is needed in following Christ. Real discipline consists of decisions to say "Yes" to Christ and "No" to self, in everyday situations.

Let us not underestimate the importance of decisions, of responsibility. The Christian way is often rocky and uphill. That is why the inspired Paul says, literally, "I beat my body black and blue and make a slave of it." Climbing the heights, weighted down by heavy baggage, is often necessary. Christianity is no "cosmic escalator," as Rufus Jones has put it. But we must struggle

> Upon the great world's *altar stairs*
> That slope through darkness up to God.

Growing souls do not ask, "Do I like to do this task? Does it contribute to my happiness?" They doggedly put one foot in front of the other and do their duty.

Perhaps at this point we should observe some of the ways we fail. Paul was concerned that after he had preached he might do a poor job of practicing. He might be "a castaway," or rejected for the prize or reward. All of us have seen people like that. Esau, Moses at Nebo, Samson, Achan, Saul, Judas, Demas, in the Bible. In my first pastorate a man in his fifties told me how much he would like to work in the church. "But," said he, "my record is such in the community that I am afraid I will do more harm than good; people do not trust me." He was a fine man, though with some "blots on the escutcheon." Later he committed suicide. Unfortunately, I was not able to recognize his reaction as depression. His failure was first within himself.

FOUR WAYS TO FAIL

We have special phrases in our language which describe the loss of self-control. We say, "He may blow up." A person may be going along doing his job fairly smoothly, in the home, at work, or in church. Suddenly, he flies off the handle, he explodes, he slashes out at someone, he blows up. Someone gets a tongue lashing. He may try to justify it by saying that it is better to express anger than to repress it, or make some similar excuse. He seems never to have heard the counsel of Proverbs: "He that is slow to anger is better than the mighty; and he that ruleth his spirit than he that taketh a city."

Another expression which describes personal failure is "fold up." When the emotional load gets heavy, he just gives up. The straw which breaks the camel's back may be a disappointment in love, a quarrel with a friend, a divorce, the loss of a job, or even a misunderstanding at church. Nothing shows our immaturity quite as clearly as frustration.

Mary was a little handicapped by her short stature. She was married, had a beautiful child, and everything seemed to be going fine. But her husband was not doing well at his job. He had been very quarrelsome lately. Added to this Mary had some surgery and was seriously ill for a few weeks. Then came the critical blow. She found evidence that he was "stepping out." What was she to do? Her husband admitted the failure and promised to behave himself in the future. But Mary's pride could not take the blow. She "folded up" and went back to her mother. A divorce followed.

A similar reaction is described by the expression, "He went off the deep end." It applies to being overcome by temptation. A man becomes involved in financial needs and "goes off the deep end" by writing hot checks or using money for himself which is not his. A woman is in love with some attractive male who is not worthy of her devotion. She refuses to recognize this and is later disappointed and becomes bitter. A man "goes off the deep end" in drink or gambling or even in his enthusiasm for some false ideology. Then, after an extended spree, it becomes much harder to rebuild his life.

A fourth form of failure is less dramatically expressed but far more frequent and more dangerous: "drifting." Someone has said, "There are a few people who make things happen, many people who watch things happen, and the overwhelming majority who have no notion of what happens." I saw the terrifying danger of this last attitude once when, in a rowboat, fishing, I almost drifted into a very powerful whirlpool. Dreaming through life does not always deal with us so excitingly. Usually, we just dawdle our time away, or we rush from one trifle to another, trying to satisfy demands which are as contradictory as lust and chastity.

Such a "drifter" came to me about eight months after he and his wife had obtained a divorce. He had been a rather good church worker until the marital trouble. Gradually he had withdrawn from his friends. He was working regularly but seemed to have lost interest. Ambition seemed to have become a weak, pointless, experience. He said to me, "I'm just spinning my wheels. My drive is gone. At one time I had great hopes for the future. Now I don't have either hopes or fears. I'm just drifting."

Of course, the people who blow up, fold up, go off the deep end, or drift, do not constitute all of the types of failures. And these experiences do not constitute the whole of life. But they are examples of not being able to manage ourselves. Who has not over-reacted to some seeming injury? And who has lived long without going through a period of marking time? The important question, it seems, is what to do when we realize that the brakes do not work or the clutch is slipping. Are we to be fatalistic and say that "what is to be will be"? Is just giving in the answer? Or, on the other hand, is the secret to "thank whatever gods may be for my unconquerable soul"? Not to wince or cry aloud is not enough. We may ache inside and finally blow our brains out.

EGO STRENGTH

The psychologist speaks of this ability to function well under strain and stress as "ego strength." He means the ability a person has within himself to face the hard facts of reality and to accept them. A weak ego has to develop ways of avoiding reality. Sometimes, it is simply shrinking from conflict. Again, it may be a complete departure from reality: one may hear voices or imagine that he is Napoleon or God. A strong ego accepts responsibility, makes constructive moves, produces the good life, and grows toward a more mature self. The ego strength is what the general public means by "will power."

Here we come face to face with the fact that only God knows how responsible a person is. This is particularly important when we try to help other people. It is easy for a wife to say to a husband, "Now, I know you can do better than that." Or for a husband to say, "All of that complaining is silly. You just think you are sick. Snap out of it and quit worrying about yourself." Quit worrying! Was ever a piece of advice more useless? All that it does usually is to add to the person's guilt-feelings and thereby increases his fears that he is inadequate. A much better method, if a husband or wife wants to be helpful, would be to say, "I love you, and I hope that you can find the forces within you to overcome this; but I will continue to love you anyway."

In this day when emotional illnesses are so prevalent the question of how to strengthen our "ego controls" is a primary one. We need all of the help we can obtain. Christianity has been working at the task of making people strong for 2000 years. The Master himself left people clothed and in their right minds. Paul wrote, "Be strong in the Lord and in the power of his might." He likened the equipment for Christian living to a Roman soldier's armor (see Eph. 6:10-17). One of his most striking phrases, "Having done all, to stand," states the aim of the life of faith; when people do what they can to change the world and then stand firm at their posts, they grow inside, and God works through them.

Perhaps, however, some suggestions about how to be "strong in the Lord" may be in order. When we are weak, how do we go about strengthening ourselves? How do we grow in self-management?

CHECK YOUR LOVE LIFE

A good place to start is in personal inventory. *Check up on your love life.* It is no accident that "Thou shalt love the Lord thy God" is the first commandment. When a person has a deep love for God he is constantly strengthened by it. It removes unnecessary fears. "Perfect love casteth out fear."

A missionary in Africa says that most of the people with whom she works are filled with fears. They are afraid of all kinds of spirits, of a world of magic and superstition. But says the missionary, we teach them that behind all these seemingly dangerous objects is a great loving Father who controls all and is always good.

How do people learn love? Not merely by having a lesson on it. Not by self-discipline. We do not tighten our belts, stick out our chins and say, "Now I'm going to love God, if it kills me." No, we learn to love by first being loved and then responding to it. Only then can it be effective in our lives and reach its fulfilment. Even God's love will mean nothing to us unless we accept it. His love gets through to us only when we recognize and respond to it. Then, as we come to understand and experience His great, eternal, sacrificial love for us, we learn to love Him more deeply and our fellow-man more unselfishly. The whole life and message of Christ was God's great revelation of His love for us. But those who refuse

Christ will never experience it, so they cannot build a deep, emotional life. We must build on the fact of God's revealed love, or we build on sand.

Then, we must let God love others through us. Only the love of God can make us go straight. If we refuse to allow that love to become the controlling force in our lives there is no hope to keep us from "acting out" our wild impulses.

There is a type of emotional disorder which many psychiatrists call "psychopathic." They also speak of the victims as being "psychopathic deviates," "constitutional psychopaths" or as having — and this is the more recent terminology — "character disorders." Such persons are not insane and not simply nervous, often not nervous at all. They merely "act out" their impulses. They write hot checks, lie, drink, use dope, and violate other moral codes. They are unstable and nonconforming. But the significant thing about every one of them is that they do not form any deep emotional attachments. They may outwardly show affection or friendliness, but they lack deep loyalties and identification with other people, which would afford stability.

A mother and father brought a nineteen-year-old boy to me. He had been writing hot checks and was doing a number of other things which were getting him in trouble. They had reared him, as best they knew, to be a good boy; but, for some reason, his loyalties did not run deep enough. No amount of persuasion seemed to help him. I said to him, "Do you ever feel sorry for what you have done and confess your sins to God?" The manner of his answer struck me. In a bright, cheerful, almost flippant voice he replied, "Oh yeah." I thought to myself, a man who really loves people and feels deeply about his sins does not answer so merrily. Finally, I had to tell his parents that the only hope for him was in deep psychological therapy, which was probably impossible outside of some institution.

The fact is, however, that all of us have some of this "acting out" trouble. Laziness is one form. Anger, dishonesty, and any other antisocial behavior patterns are all in this class. The cure for those of us who are not seriously impaired — in which case, the help of a specialist is needed — is to deepen our emotional attachments. Any other approach is symptom treatment only; we need to deal with the cause. Love is the real treatment. We need to love God and to love our fellows with pure, unbreakable, all-giving, and all-forgiving love. To grow in this kind of love is an obvious need for all of us, and a possibility.

ADMIT CHARACTER DEFECTS

A second approach to self-management is this: *We must admit our character defects.* Preachers and teachers may hold up high standards of good behavior, but mental assent to these is not enough. We must face ourselves and say, "Thou ailest there and there and there."

Too often we think of sin as event, while actually it is always a personal act or decision. Some people think that confession of sin means to recount the episodes in which we did wrong and admit that we were there, even involved. I doubt that rehearsing our failures in confession of our sins to God does us any good or pleases God. It seems to me that true confession involves more than that. We need to ask ourselves, "Why did I tell that lie or fall into that habit or refuse that job that I was asked to do? What is wrong with my character that I have failed in that respect?"

This is involved in what the New Testament means by repentance and cross-bearing. In repentance, a person gets a new mind about his conduct. He not only sees that he committed a wrong act, but he admits that the reason he did it was because he had the wrong attitude toward God. That is why the Bible speaks of "repentance toward God." And when Jesus said, "If any man will come after me . . . let him take up his cross daily," He was calling us to accept the hard aspects of life. Crosses are to die on. As we accept the frustration of resisting temptation, we die to infantilism and become adult.

It takes courage to face our real defects and to ask God to change us. We know that in the very act of prayer we must accept responsibility for making right decisions. We must cooperate with God if He is to help us. Sometimes this means accepting and living with anxiety. There is no escaping conflict. In other words, we cannot save our faces and save our souls (or grow spiritually) at the same time.

LIVE IN THE PRESENT

A third force in strengthening our skill at self-direction is to *learn to act in the present.*

Everyone has met the elderly person who is turning all his thoughts back to childhood: "When I was a boy, etc." "I remember just as well as if it was yesterday the time when . . ." and then a long harangue about "the good old days." No one wishes to be unkind to those for whom memories of childhood events have become so vivid, but living in the past is a poor tonic for spiritual growth. It is a way of rubbing yourself in on yourself, and those about you are not very interested in the process.

On the other hand, many young people and some others are eternal dreamers. Tomorrow they will pray more, become great Christians, do the heroic deed, make a reputation. But today they fail to study, neglect to read, use only half of their brain power. They do not realize that people who wake up to find themselves famous or successful or great saints usually haven't been asleep. All of us are like Scarlett O'Hara in *Gone with the Wind* when she said, "I won't think about that today. I'll do something about it tomorrow."

Of course, human beings cannot blot out their memories any more than they can refrain from fearing the future at times. But we can grab the reins of our minds and say, "Whoa, I have today on my hands now; my present obligation is to live it well." Sir William Osler, the great Christian physician, used to talk about living in "day-tight compartments." He said that we need to undress our souls at night like we do our bodies. Alcoholics Anonymous members talk about beginning the day by praying to God and saying, "I may drink the rest of my life; I cannot promise; but today, help me to stay completely free of drink this day." Then, at the close of the day, they thank Him for victory.

This is what great Christians have always done. They live in a state of constant responsibility. Others may take time out, declare moral holidays, make exceptions, but we know that to do so is to turn our backs upon God and to regress. God must work through us. But He does so as we acknowledge at any given time that we are "under God" and must depend upon His help.

Just before Jesus went back to the Father, Peter pointed to John and said, "Master, what about this man? What do you want him to do?" Jesus was almost severe when He answered, in effect, "If it is my will that he stay on this earth until I come again, what is that to you? You follow me for yourself!" (John 21:20-23). It is the old story of thinking of finding God's will in a long-range life program. What He says to us is that if we would find His will it must be in the proper management of our lives one day at a time.

CHAPTER ELEVEN

When Temptation Comes

Some people say that opportunity knocks at our door just once. That may be true. But temptation bangs away persistently all the days of your life. Or, to change the figure a bit, there are three schools in which every person must enroll if he lives long on this earth. They are: work, temptation, and suffering. William James once said, "No man has matriculated in the university of life until he has been well tempted."

But there is a great difference between being tempted and falling. Paul, in 1 Corinthians 10:12-13, said, in substance: "So the man who thinks he stands securely must be on the lookout not to fall. No temptation has taken hold of you but what is common to human nature. And God is to be trusted not to let you be tempted beyond your strength, but when temptation comes, to make a way out of it, so that you can bear up under it."

This passage presents three important facts about temptation. First, all of us are in danger all the time. Second, no person ever faces a superhuman temptation; we have such choices as our fellow human beings have, no greater and no less — that which is "common to human nature." Third, we are not in this battle alone. God, in His providence, determines how many fiery darts He allows Satan to throw at us in a given day. Our Father does not promise to keep us from being tempted; it is His aim to keep us from falling.

CHRISTIANS MUST MEET TEMPTATION

One of the great lessons of the Christian life is learning how to meet temptation. It is doubtful that we can ever learn much about it in church; for we learn by experience. But, on the other hand, we need to profit by whatever insight is given in God's Word. If each life had to start from scratch and learn everything over, the race would never have gone beyond the Stone Age. Whatever else the Bible is, it is the accumulated wisdom about man's spiritual life. I believe that it is more; it is God's revelation concerning human nature, life, death, eternity, and especially about God Himself.

But you would think that nothing has ever been learned about temptation, on the basis of the way so many people live. All of us are weaker and are more often failures than we ought to be. Why? We have turned our backs upon the guidance which God has given us. Not only have we invited temptations into our lives, but we have also given them plush chairs to sit on. Sure, we have said, "Get behind me, Satan," but often under our breaths we have added, "and push." Sometimes we have closed both eyes to sin, and again we have merely winked at it. Or, worse still, we joke about temptation. Many of us have quoted in fun the words of Oscar Wilde, "I can resist everything except temptation." So many of us are just pilgrims on the path of least resistance.

Yet, most of us are serious in our intent to resist what we really believe to be wrong. We may joke about some practices which fanatics get excited about, but all of us know that life is frail and that human values can easily become distorted. And temptation is primarily a religious concept, like sin. We may suffer conflict between our drives and the tribal rules without religious faith, but temptation is the conflict we feel between doing what we want to do and what God reveals as His will. Temptation, then, is the tendency within a person to have his own way and follow his own inclinations rather than follow the revealed will of God. In this sense, only Christians and those struggling with the Christian message can be tempted.

TEMPTATION DECEIVES

The next significant point about temptation is that its chief characteristic is not surprise but deception.

We all like to pretend that our sins slip up on us, that suddenly we are attacked from ambush. But this is not true. Of course some people who are not particularly bright may not see what is happening to them until it has already occurred. A moron will often get himself into a compromising position because he has not understood the direction in which he was moving. It is also true that people of all types are suddenly *caught* in sin, but this does not mean that they were tempted suddenly. They may have been going on in sin for a long while, and then all at once it comes out into the open. Karl Menninger said "People never slip into trouble. They march into it."

Yes, usually a person goes very deliberately into sin. In fact, contrary to what the public generally thinks, a person usually has to work at the matter of overcoming his inhibitions and making himself fall into grievous sin. Perhaps this is a much stronger reason for the presence of sin in many lives than most of us realize. Sin becomes a challenge. We see the forbidden fruit and know that we are allowed only to look at it. This becomes a challenge to us to assert ourselves and prove that we are not hampered by the rules and laws which some people consider important.

But the really big element in sin is deception. We are blinded to temptation because we tell ourselves that the evil deed is not really so bad. There is a certain blindness always attached to traveling on the road to evil. As a modern novelist and essayist, Aldous Huxley, says in *Eyeless in Gaza:* "Men don't tell themselves that the wrong they are doing is wrong.

Either they do it without thinking, or else they invent reasons for believing it is right."

Adam and Eve no doubt assured themselves that even if they were making a mistake, it would not be of any great consequence. Lot pitched his tent toward Sodom and later found himself in the very middle of the city, living very much as the people lived. Achan must have minimized the temptation to keep the "goodly Babylonish garment." David thought that because he was a king, he could ignore the principles of justice and honor to steal his neighbor's wife. In every case of temptation there is the element of deception. It is difficult to keep from being hoodwinked when the world has worked out so many easy rationalizations: "One time won't matter," "Everybody is doing it," "The majority can't be wrong," "Come on and be a good sport," "I'm just human."

The element of deception is particularly noticeable when someone is trying to quit a sin. Here is a man who has a good resolution. He swears by all that is high and holy that he is going to quit gambling or drinking, that he is going to quit after one more fling. This one time will be his last. When you hear a man say that, you may be sure that he is deceiving himself. I would much rather risk a man's quitting who says, "I may have gambled every other day of my life, but tonight I shall leave it alone." This man is overcoming his craving at least for the time being. The other tells himself that he is a good man, else he would not have such good resolutions; therefore he can afford to indulge himself one more time. He becomes quite a hero to himself, and yet his craving is destroying him because he is giving it one more chance.

OUR OWN EVIL DESIRES ALLURE US

This leads us to another point: that temptation springs from within us and springs from an inevitable disparity between our desires and the will of God. Emil Brunner writes with discernment: "Man who has not yet perceived that evil is entwined in the very roots of his personality has a superficial personality."

The Apostle James had the same thing in mind when he wrote: "Blessed is the man who endures trial, for when he has stood the test he will receive the crown of life which God has promised to those who love him. Let no one say when he is tempted, 'I am tempted by God,' for God cannot be tempted with evil and He Himself tempts no one. But each person is tempted when he is lured and enticed by his own desire. Then desire when it has conceived gives birth to sin; and sin when it is full-grown, it brings forth death" (James 1:12-15 Williams).

Do you remember Satan's words to Adam and Eve? He appealed both to their pride and to their physical nature: "If you eat this fruit, you will be as gods, knowing good and evil." And then even though God had said to Adam and Eve, "Ye shall not eat of it, neither shall ye touch it, lest ye die," the woman saw that the tree was good for food and that it was pleasant to the eye. The appeal both to pride and to physical desire is an appeal to that which is within all of us. As someone has said, "Honest bread is very well — it's the butter that makes the temptation." The incentive is usually external, but the motive is basic to our very structure.

THE TEMPTATION OF JESUS

Satan's first trial of Jesus was an appeal to satisfy the natural drive in other than God-given ways. Hunger is natural; it is a God-given desire. But when the devil suggested that the satisfaction for hunger be achieved in the prostitution of His divine powers, it became a temptation. So, in many of our temptations we have the suggestion of satisfying a normal, wholesome desire in an abnormal and antisocial manner.

The second temptation, to leap down from the Temple, was a temptation to turn religion into magic. This has been offered over and over through the ages. Many people want religion to produce for them some uncanny results. They want to talk in unknown tongues, or go off into trances, or have God perform a miracle at every turn of the way.

The third temptation was one to justify the means for the end. Jesus had come to set up a kingdom. Satan offered to achieve that good end by means that were unholy. Communism makes a similar offer today on a large scale. At one time prominent Americans were saying of Italian fascism: "After all, if it gets results, what does it matter if a few people are destroyed and principles are violated? The results are what matter." Jesus condemned such reasoning in His trial before He began his public ministry.

Everyone Has Weak Moments

These aspects of temptation we have been discussing point to one great fact of our nature — that every man has his weak spots and his weak moments. Some of us have an immunity to certain temptations that do not interest us. As the old French proverb says, "We fall to the side to which we lean." Then again, all of us are stronger at times than at others; we have more resistance. We do not take a cold, either, every time we meet that determined little virus. But wait till some day when we have cold feet! The devil, sly person that he is, knows when to present his sly suggestions and at what point we can be wooed. He knows that every man has an Achilles' heel, and that is the point for successful attack.

This demands of us that we be constantly on our guard. Too many of us have been like the little girl who said, "God, help me to be good, but don't fence me in." We do not like the bitter fact of moral decisions. Indeed, someone has said, with a great deal of insight, that the thing that makes temptation really hard to resist is the fact that we may never have the chance again. When the opportunity for pleasure or for compromise or for making ourselves big at the expense of others is presented to us, we are strongly inclined to avail ourselves of this chance to do wrong. Conflict is inevitable. Paul expressed it in these words, "The good that I would I do not: but the evil which I would not, that I do." It is expressed many times in proverbs such as: "Whatsoever a man soweth that shall he also reap," "Chickens will come home to roost," and "You cannot have your cake and eat it too."

HELP IN OVERCOMING TEMPTATION

Certainly every serious-minded person wants to overcome temptation. We are taught to pray, "Lead us not into temptation, but deliver us from evil." It is literally a prayer that says, "Do not allow me to be led into temptations that are too strong for me, but help me to overcome the evil one." And God's Word is full of suggestions about how to overcome evil and of insight into the very nature of evil. Perhaps the reason more of us do not read the Bible is because we are afraid of the help that it will give us. We are afraid that we will be deprived of the pleasure connected with our ignorance. As the book review turned in by the freshman English student said, "This book contains more information about penguins than I am interested in knowing about." Yet if we would read the Word of God, we would hear Paul say in his letter to the Ephesians, "Put on the whole armor of God, that ye may be able to stand against the wiles of the devil." And then Paul proceeds to describe this armor and how it can help those who are willing to accept it.

Someone has said that no one becomes a saint in his sleep. William Thackeray wrote steadily for eight years before he gained any prominence. When a critic remarked that he woke up at the end of that time to find himself famous, someone remarked, "When a man wakes up to find himself a success as a writer, he has not been asleep."

Temptation today is as it was in the garden of Eden: it is ever present in our lives. The tree on which hung the forbidden fruit was in the midst of the garden — just at the point where all the walks converged, where Adam and Eve had to pass it every day. This is a parable of life.

Two essential means for withstanding and overcoming the temptations of Satan and the forces of evil within and without are honesty and prayer.

BE THOROUGHLY HONEST

Three possible ways are open to us in handling the evil with which our lives are confronted. The first is that of indulgence. Many people feel that the only way to handle their impulses is to act them out. The second is repression. Those who follow this method not only take their stand against the impulse, but they also deny that they have the impulse. This method leads to emotional illnesses of many sorts and to moral distortion. The third way is suppression of the impulse. This is a constructive fight against the impulse and does not attempt to deny that we have the desire to violate the laws of God and man in self-indulgence. Rather, it faces the hard realization that some impulses must be thwarted in order for us to become our best. It demands complete honesty.

Jesus met His temptations head on. He did not postpone them or run away from them. He did not let the impact of Satan's suggestions pile up on Him. Rather, in the three temptations, which we have already discussed, immediately upon their suggestion He had an answer from the Word of God. When Satan spoke through Simon Peter to try to turn Jesus aside from His dying for our sins, immediately Jesus said, "Get thee behind me, Satan." And in Gethsemane never once did He deny the alternative with which He was faced. He said, "If thy will cannot be done without my death, I am ready to go."

All of us know how difficult it is to be thoroughly honest.

We give ourselves alibis for the wrong we have done and reasons for taking further chances. Adam would have been thinking something like this: "The woman whom thou gavest to be with me, she gave me of the tree, and I did eat. How could I have turned down her whom thou didst make so attractive, the supreme glory of thy creative fingers? She told me that I ought to eat, that it was good for me. She had tasted it. Who was I to embarrass her by refusing, to doubt her wisdom by telling her it was a mistake, to repudiate the risk she herself had taken? That would have been discourteous, ungallant — and she is a charmer. Who would not want to comply with a request or persuasion made by so lovely a creature? Don't you see, God, you sort of put me on the spot. You ought not to chide me. The fault is with the temptation and the tempter."

Over and over men and women have found excuses. Sometimes it has been heredity, environment, human nature, the deception and unfairness of other people. We all have our scapegoats. When Aaron was asked about the golden calf he had made while Moses was on Sinai receiving the law, he said, "I cast it [the gold] into the fire, and there came out this calf." He used an alibi and was weakened. Hambone said concerning an alibi: "An alibi is the thing you tell your wife to convince her you was at the prayer meeting where you wasn't when you was at the crap game where you was."

Ask God for Help

The other suggestion for overcoming temptation is simply that of prayer. Many who have not been able to explain how the victory came have asked God for help and have received it. At the very heart of all our temptations in the presence of evil is that presumptuousness which keeps us from getting on our knees and asking God for aid.

The writer of Hebrews insisted, however, that we should not be timid about asking God for help, for He is eager to hear our plea in the hour of need. "For we have not a high priest which cannot be touched with the feeling of our infirmities; but was in all points tempted like as we are, yet without sin. Let us therefore come boldly unto the throne of grace, that we may obtain mercy, and find grace to help in time of need" (Heb. 4: 15-16).

The story is told of a textile factory in which was found this sign on the wall over each machine: "If your threads get tangled, send for the foreman." A new employee went to work, and soon the threads became badly tangled. The more she attempted to untangle them, the more helpless she became. By and by, in desperation, after wasting a lot of time, she did call for help. When the foreman came, he asked her why she had not sent for him earlier. She replied in self-defense, "I did my best." He answered with a smile, "Remember, doing your best is sending for me."

There are times when life becomes very difficult and all the threads get tangled. Temptations press from many sides, and the buttresses from within seem about to crumble. In such times we should remember that we have never tried until we have tried God. In the words of Paul, if I may paraphrase them, "Our temptations are all common ones." We may feel that we are weaker than our neighbor or that more suggestions of evil come just to us. But the fact is that God is testing us, and He is controlling the pressure that any given temptation can put upon us. He will make a way for us to win if we only look to Him. There is always a way out with Him, so "put on the whole armor of God." Surrender your whole nature to Him. This is the best safeguard.

CHAPTER TWELVE

The Man in the Basement

Did you ever go down into an old fashioned basement of a house and look at the accumulation of the years? I am not thinking of the modern basements with recreation rooms and bars. The old basements in large homes were the storerooms for such things as baby high chairs, trunks, empty fruit jars, broken rocking chairs, old bedsteads, family heirlooms, discarded family portraits, camping equipment, dog harnesses, and parts of many things from many places.

If you walk around with a flashlight in your hand in such a basement, your mind is crowded with a hundred associated memories. Some of the objects might bring tears, some laughter, some a wry smile. As the spotlight falls on each object, you remember things and events which have long been shelved in your mind. Some of them, perhaps, you would like to forget. Some bring back very tender and cherished memories. We are a part of all we have met.

I am thinking that in every person there is something that corresponds roughly to a basement. It is a part of us, just as the basement is a part of the house. We may not be aware of what is in this part of ourselves, but it is there just the same. It is related to ourselves and our past. The real difference is that this part of us is not like old broken rockers and fishing tackle — still and unobtrusive; this part of us is dynamic, alive, and constantly giving us trouble. The man in the basement knocks on the door to get out, steals through the basement windows, and demands constant watching.

FREUD AND PAUL

The importance of our secret self was first brought forcefully to my attention years ago when I read, from the pen of Halford Luccock of Yale Divinity School, the statement that the Viennese psychologist, Sigmund Freud, was probably "closer to Paul than any other modern writer, including all the theologians." Both emphasized the constant and necessary war within the personality. Both saw the deep, disturbing depravity of man. Both saw that life consists of adjustments which the individual makes in the midst of conflict.

Freud was not a Christian, but as a scientist he arrived at this sort of a view of man. We come into the world equipped with certain instincts or drives or motivating forces. The little baby does not know the difference between himself and "the other than himself." He has all sorts of drives: tenderness, hunger, anger, curiosity, and so on. The child is extremely selfish and demanding. As he grows from infancy, he finds that these crude desires must be conditioned. He must become civilized.

The civilizing force within the personality is the conscience or super-ego. It is a kind of judge or super-parent who says, "Thou shalt not" or "Thou shalt." It is more, actually. In the process of life development the conscience not only forbids a deed but even denies that such a desire is present. At least, some force within the personality holds down the impulses both by conscious effort and by unconscious denial.

Many people think that religion is allied with the conscience, so they spend their lives trying to obey rules and to make other people obey them. The revelation of God, to them, is the revelation of His will — as in the Ten Commandments for example. Such people have little mercy or goodness. They spend their lives trying to be good, and nobody believes in their goodness except themselves.

Between the conscience and the instincts or impulses, for Freud and most contemporary psychologists, is the conscious self. The ego, it is called. It consists of will-power, reason, and love, the really human and good part of man. The conscious self serves as a kind of arbiter between the lower self and the higher self or conscience. What we are, they say, depends on ego strength, upon the self-directing, thinking, deciding part of the human personality.

Now a great part of this whole process of the individual's behavior is unconscious. Most of the instinctual life is. A part of the conscience is. The mind is like an iceberg, nine-tenths of it under water and one-tenth visible to the human eye. Thus, there is much of mystery in all of us.

At the Yale School of Alcohol Studies a member of the class asked this question of a well-known psychiatrist: "Dr. Tiebout, if the human personality is somewhat as you describe, isn't an understanding of the unconscious and an acceptance and conscious control of our impulses all we need?" Dr. Tiebout's reply was, "God pity the man who thinks he understands his unconscious." He went on to show how the alcoholic, like anyone else, needs a Power greater than himself to manage his complex personality.

You see, religion aims at the conscious self. It is not on the side of the conscience as is commonly supposed. It is on the side of the ego. It aims at building a balanced person, at strengthening controls which do not leave him weak or in the thick of battle constantly, but help him make an adjustment which enables him to give his life in service to God and man.

The key words of the Christian faith are peace, joy, freedom, love, truth, and faith. But the first three can never be achieved as long as either the instinct or the conscience is in control. It is only as love for other people, the truth of God as

revealed in Christ, and a faith-surrender to Him become domi-
nant in our lives that we are free and, at the same time,
controlled.

MENTAL ILLNESS

By way of parenthesis, I should like to point out also that
mental illness, which is such a great problem in our day, is
not a sign of badness or lack of faith. Illness occurs when the
normal, automatic ego controls are not working well. The
conflict between the impulses and the conscience is not being
handled properly. It may be that the conscience is too severe
(for it is not trustworthy), or the childish desires too strong,
or the conscious organization of the personality faulty through
ignorance or lack of love. In any case, to judge a person who
is emotionally ill is contrary to both science and religion.

For example, a young doctor told one of my students that
he had never seen a real Christian on a psychiatric ward. That
is the height of prejudice and stupidity! Some of the best people I have ever known have had emotional disorders. And I
have seen some great Christians who were temporarily insane.
People become mentally ill when their repressions get out of
hand or their method of personality organization is not successful. To blame the person for that is unkind, unwarranted,
and unchristian.

What, then, is the approach of religion to handling this
problem of living with ourselves? It is twofold. The Christian faith tries to acquaint man with his true nature and to
persuade him to allow God to help him manage it. As stated
before, put in modern terms, religion aims at the conscious
self. This self must deal with many problems which grow
out of the instinctual drives, or the unconscious; but also with
an equal number which grow out of the scoldings or pamper-
ings of a distorted conscience. It is the conscious self which is
responsible to God and can be judged by God only; which

can be born again and grow into Christlikeness. How God performs these miracles, no one can fully explain. But the whole problem of salvation and Christianity is bringing this man in the basement under control and into cooperation with God.

JESUS ON HUMAN NATURE

Read the words of Jesus on this subject: "And he said, 'What comes out of a man is what defiles a man. For from within, out of the heart of man, come evil thoughts, fornication, theft, murder, adultery, coveting, wickedness, deceit, licentiousness, envy, slander, pride, foolishness. All these evil things come from within, and they defile a man'" (Mark 7:20-23 RSV).

This passage grew out of a defense Jesus was offering for His disciples. They were not observing all of the Jewish ceremonial cleansing rituals, such as washing the hands to the elbows before eating — this was before the day of information about microbes, so was purely a religious ritual. The Master's attitude was extremely radical, in the light of His times. But the important part of the defense, for us, is His list of the evils which sprang from within the human heart. He was saying that moral failures are more important than ceremonial failures. They are what really harm the human personality, "defile man"; and the human spirit is God's chief concern.

Look at the names He gives to these destructive traits. Evil thoughts mean the planning of evil without regard to God's will, as in David's dealing with Bathsheba. Fornication and adultery apply to sexual immorality, and licentiousness to "over-sexuality." "Murder" and "theft" are obvious. Coveting is the itch to have more, the "have more" attitude, and grows out of a response to a corrupt culture. Wickedness is just plain meanness and probably designates what moderns would call "criminality." Deceit is another kind of criminality — dishonesty in business — it may even apply to social deception.

An evil eye is the sin of jealousy in a highly competitive society. Slander is the product of a vicious tongue used in some way to hurt someone else. Pride is holding oneself above others and above what God intended. And, finally, foolishness is an anticlimactic word which probably includes most of the others; it means having no moral sense.

This list of sins is quite inclusive. All of them are antisocial ones and bring suffering and sorrow in their wake. Jesus' concept of what defiles man is a far cry from the useless religious rules and compulsive rituals of the Jews of His day. Not one of these sins has to do with ceremony or religious dogma. And the point which we must not overlook is that these debasing patterns of living come from within. They spring from human nature; they are rooted in the very egoistic structure of our infantile selves.

A little five-year-old boy, the child of a friend, surprised his parents and his neighbors by hitting a neighbor boy in the head with a rock. He was frightened and ashamed. His explanation was: "Daddy, I don't know how to explain it, but this is the way it happened. A voice seemed to say to me, 'Go ahead and throw it'; and another voice, 'Don't do it,' and somehow I went ahead and threw it." His father was rather firm in his objection to the voice theory, but it is a very old one. However, the Bible puts it this way: "Every man is tempted, when he is drawn away of his own lust, and enticed" (James 1:14).

This is no attempt to say that man is all bad. Rather, it states frankly that evil does not spring simply from one's culture or from bad social patterns, but from the very center of each individual life.

PAUL'S VIEW OF THE FLESH

A similar concept is presented by the Apostle Paul in his letter to the Galatians. Here he contrasts the struggle of the spirit against the "flesh." It is fairly evident from reading this letter, or the one to the Romans, that by "Spirit" the writer does not mean simply "our higher selves" but the Holy Spirit. This is clear when we remember that the Spirit of God dwells in every true Christian; he has been born of the Spirit and made a member of the body of Christ.

So Paul says that the flesh is the mainspring of evil. Marshall points out that by flesh Paul means "what we mean today when we speak of the natural impulses and instincts which, while they are not sinful in themselves, master us and become occasions of sin unless we master them." Or more accurately, they master us when we are cut off from the redeeming power of God.

But how does the flesh express itself? Paul says that "the works of the flesh are plain: immorality, impurity, licentiousness, idolatry, sorcery, enmity, strife, jealousy, anger, selfishness, dissension, party spirit, envy, drunkenness, carousing, and the like. I warn you, as I warned you before, that those who do such things shall not inherit the kingdom of God" (Gal. 5:19-21 RSV).

A close look at this list of fourteen bad behavior patterns shows that they may easily fall into four classes: (1) sex; (2, false religion; (3) hostility; and (4) intemperance. The first three obviously apply to irresponsibility in sex life. The next two concern all sorts of heathen practices which put images and magic as a prominent part of religion. The third group includes the largest list of sins (eight), and all are a violation of the spirit of love; they have to do with what we speak of today as interpersonal or human relations. The fourth, which includes the last two items on the list, are both words which apply to group drinking. In their social structure there probably was no "solo" drinking, as we have in our Western culture. In any case, the drinking led to intoxication which needs no argument to prove its degrading effect.

As Dr. A. T. Robertson says, this is "a lively list" of sins. Lively and earthy, and it is interesting to note that the Roman Catholic official list of "seven deadly sins" includes two, "gluttony" and "laziness," which are not included in either of these. I prefer Jesus' and Paul's.

But to call these "lists of sins" is almost to miss the point. They are more nearly attempts to tell the nature of man by suggesting how he acts. You tell what is in a well by the kind of liquid the pump produces. Some of us would like to divorce ourselves from our natures, jump out of our skins, and blame our sins on Satan, on our parents who represent our early training, or on our culture. This seems like very superficial psychology and anthropology to me. As Emil Brunner points out, "Christian anthropology regards man as not only responsible but also as guilty." He is "neither animal nor divine."

It would be easy for some of us to agree with Jesus' and Paul's description of human nature and say that "there are a lot of people in the world like that." Like the woman who said to the preacher, "Wonderful sermon! Everything you said applies to somebody or other I know."

Look Around and Within

As we look closely, however, at ourselves, our neighbors, and even at our families, we find some of these same characteristics present. Is any one of us free from covetousness or envy or pride or selfishness? H. G. Wells, in *The Holy Terror,* writes: "Man has become a new animal who can jump a hundred miles, see through a brick wall, bombard the atom, and analyse the stars, yet he goes on behaving like the weak, quarrelsome ape he used to be." Bishop Creighton has said, "Whenever you have got the ape and the tiger out of people there still remains the donkey, a much more stubborn animal." We speak of our "animal natures," but we must not forget that they are a part of ourselves. It may be that they are the part of us to which Shakespeare referred in the thirty-first sonnet, "Things removed, that hidden in thee lie."

Perhaps we can see this part of ourselves more clearly if we translate what Paul called "the flesh" into modern terms. The man in the basement is dealt with in modern psychology as well as in the Bible. But even the language of the child may describe him. Such a prominent part of reality does not need technical language to contain it.

CHARACTERISTICS OF THE SECRET SELF

The man in the basement is *a selfish child*. Dr. Leon Saul says that "within every grown-up lives the little child he once was." This is no reflection on children. It is natural for them to make demands, to attempt to dominate, to seek pleasure only, to be jealous, to act out their impulses. But this self-centered, I-want-my-way, why-doesn't-someone-love-me attitude is within everyone of us from the bassinet to the mortuary.

This secret self is also *a killer*. Some of the most saintly people I have ever known, when they were hurt deeply, hated violently. They may cover it up with politeness or camouflage it with coldness, but it is hate just the same. "The urge to kill" is deep within every human being. A little child will say, "I hate you; I could kill you." An older person reacts to the same murderous impulse by fearing another will die. It is a fact borne out by many clinical studies that great anxiety concerning another's death is often caused by an unconscious wish that he might die. Likewise suicide is often shown to be the result of hostility toward someone else that gets turned inward toward the self.

This baby, basement self seeks, under all circumstances, to *avoid pain*. "Don't hurt me" is its slogan. Therefore, when this self is in control, the individual never has the courage to stand for something. He had rather be "an innocent bystander." Religion to him is an escape, and he will not accept any other. No crosses for him, unless someone else dies on it, like Christ. The path of least resistance is the royal road to heaven for him. If he suffers, he takes a drink to relax him. He "passes the buck," but he never bucks the line. "O please go 'way and let me sleep" is his theme song.

Quite an unexpected, and very subtle, bit of unconscious behavior — at least, springing from the unconscious — is *humor*. The man in the basement laughs at the man upstairs (the conscience). Humor is the mercy the conscience shows to the fleshly self. We laugh at those who kick over the traces. Which side are we on? The side of morality or of sin? Everyone knows that sexy jokes "lay them in the aisles" — some audiences, at least; even some very nice people. For the moment of laughter we are identified with the "superior" viewpoint which is unmoral, and we show mercy to our instincts. That is why humor is one of the most revealing facts about an individual. Only really good people can afford to laugh. For the remainder, it dulls the edge of moral discrimination. Good humor, then, is a blessing, in that we all need some mercy. But bad humor is either vulgar, cruel, vindictive, or downright silly.

Finally, the man in the basement is *burning up with ambition*. He intends to get ahead, God or no God. His associates are competitors instead of collaborators. His way of life is rivalism instead of mutualism. James and John, coming to Jesus, asking to sit "one on thy right hand, and the other on the left" in His kingdom, are a perfect illustration. Their egocentric selves were in charge during this interview. The will to power even enters into religion and is sometimes very difficult to discern.

Now what has this picture of man's inner, lower, impulsive self to do with growth? Does it matter what we think about the flesh or the heart? Our interest is not in an analysis of the nature or essence of man, as much as it is in understanding how he behaves. In modern jargon, we are concerned about "what makes him tick." This leads inevitably to a concept of what man is in himself. And can anyone observe his neighbors and question the realism of the New Testament?

How Growth Takes Place

Growth, then, is concerned with progress in dealing with these objectionable impulses. This world is a very hard place for a "baby" who never becomes an adult. When people "act out" their impulses or hold on to childish patterns of living, they are headed for sorrow and distress. The viewpoint of the New Testament, it seems, is that salvation does not deliver a person from the fleshly self. Nor does it propose simply to strengthen his conscience so that he may "hold down," by fear and inhibitions, the wild desires — keep the basement door shut, so to speak. This cannot be done. Growth consists in the strengthening of our conscious controls.

Christ allies Himself with the ego or conscious self. His is not a religion of rules and punishment, like Judaism and Mohammedanism, as well as popular paganism. Nor is it an escapism into mystic trances or separation from the world. To go further, Christ does not propose to transform or redeem the unconscious, as E. Stanley Jones and some others claim. All one has to do to know that a Christian's unconscious is not redeemed is to examine his dreams, or watch him become insane, or even catch him off guard when he is frustrated. The unconscious takes over in these cases. Christ saves the whole person, of course, but the unconscious or impulsive life is not destroyed. It is held down, controlled by the Spirit of God working through the Christian. We must learn to live with the man in the basement and keep him under control. Growth is the increasingly smooth control of that aggressive, untamed part of self.

The Christian View

What is the Christian solution to handling the instinctual self? I believe that there is a divine way and there is a human way. The human way includes indulgence, will-power, self-destruction (as in Buddhism), and auto-suggestion (the "positive thinking" relaxation cults). But the Christian way is one of dependence upon God, from start to finish. No mental tricks, no mysterious rituals. It seems to be contained in three experiences which I shall merely mention.

The first one is "death." "And those who belong to Christ Jesus have crucified the flesh with its passions and desires" (Gal. 5:24 RSV). "Put to death therefore what is earthly in you: immorality, impurity, passion, evil desire, and covetousness, which is idolatry" (Col. 3:5 RSV). Other passages might be quoted but these state clearly the Christian view.

Well, one says, if we are to "crucify the flesh," let us get busy and destroy the man in the basement. Yes, let us! But like the proverbial cat, he has a number of lives. We can never quite destroy him. These death figures are symbols of the experience the Christian has of bringing himself to Christ, unconscious and all, and saying, "Here I am; I renounce all loyalties except to you; you may have the keys to all of the rooms of my house; cause me to die to sin but to live unto righteousness." Or something like that. At any rate, a cross is involved. We accept this death concept just as we do the words of our Master, "Be ye therefore perfect, even as your Father which is in heaven is perfect." In fact, they are two sides of the same experience.

The second aspect of dealing with our drives is to accept the conflict. Those who do not wish to live in conflict are not made for this world. Paul describes his own "struggle of the soul" in Romans 7: "I do not understand my own actions. For I do not do what I want, but I do the very thing I hate. Now if I do what I do not want, I agree that the law is good. So then it is no longer I that do it, but sin which dwells within me. For I know that nothing good dwells within me, that is, in my flesh. I can will what is right, but I cannot do it. For I do not do the good I want, but the evil I do not want is what I do. Now if I do what I do not want, it is no longer I that do it, but sin which dwells within me" (Rom. 7:15-20 RSV). He concludes the passage by thanking God for the victory through Jesus Christ. The Christian wins, but he never destroys the foe.

There are stories of ancient tyrants who forced those guilty of murder to suffer an offensive punishment. The dead body was chained to the murderer in such a way that he was forced to bear it until it had completely rotted away. This may have been what Paul had in mind when he said, "Wretched man that I am! Who will deliver me from this body of death?" (Rom. 7:24 RSV).

It is at the point of struggling with the flesh that religion and psychiatry meet. Both are interested in strengthening the ego or conscious self. Psychiatry deals with people whose conscious controls are more seriously impaired; they are emotionally sick.

Let us illustrate it this way. A certain clinical psychologist states that the unconscious forces may be likened to a large number of rats in a basement. All openings are closed except one from the basement to the kitchen. If we allow them to come out one at a time, we may be able to kill them. But if a number rush through the opening at once we are overwhelmed, confused, and disturbed. If for some reason he has to face too many decisions, too much unconscious material comes through, his anxiety greatly increases, he must seek ways of defending himself, and thereby becomes sick.

Religion does not propose to cure insanity any more than it does cancer or tuberculosis, but it aids. Actually, the right kind of religion, one that is realistic, intelligent, and loving, may do a great deal to strengthen the ego. It has been doing it for centuries. That is why it has been called "the psychiatry of the masses." But, unless the conscious controls are broken, man is responsible to God for "living in conflict" and making such decisions as he is capable of making. Only people who have a great deal of "struggle" are good Christians in God's sight. In other words, since our "enemies" are constant, we must either stay on the firing line or sink into complacency and spiritual inertia. Those who are fighting in the Christian manner are growing.

THE SPIRIT AND THE FLESH

The final insight into successful control of the flesh is to live by the Spirit. "Practice living by the Spirit and then by no means will you gratify the cravings of the lower nature" (Gal. 5:16 Williams). Herbert Spencer has well said, "You cannot get golden conduct out of leaden instincts." Most of us do about as well as we may be expected to do without God's help. But the point here is that we need not be without His help. When we become Christians by the creative act of God's Spirit, we have just begun. The secret of growth in spiritual living is to be found in conscious dependence on the Holy Spirit, just as we depend on a strong parental hand to lead us when we are young.

The theologian has little advantage over the novice in understanding how God leads us. Both must learn by experience, and this comes about by a humble soul opening itself to God as a flower opens to the sunshine and fresh air. In ways that cannot be analyzed or explained, God gives strength, aids judgment, suggests new pathways. Our task is to learn to follow his leading, as the leaf follows the breeze.

I do not believe that anyone, psychologist or any other, can tell exactly how "living by the Spirit" strengthens the character and personality. It is evident, however, to anyone who has closely observed the development of sincere Christians that real stamina comes to those who follow this technique. There are times when such Christians are not sure which promptings come from the Holy Spirit and which from their own unconscious. But their very seeking and asking for God's help is itself both a growth stimulus and the result of growth. It clips the wings of pride and builds a bulwark against the onslaught of temptation. "For as many as are led by the Spirit of God, they are the sons of God" (Rom. 8:14).

CHAPTER THIRTEEN

Getting Along With People

Every man is a problem in search of a solution. We are born into a world that is autocratic. That is, from the very first we are pushed around, given orders, bossed, made to conform. And the child's problem is to learn how to move from an autocratic world to a democratic one. We must learn how to boss ourselves instead of being bossed — and it is a slow, painful process. Children grow only as they learn how to solve problems which are gradually pitched into their laps.

Learning to get along with people is one problem with which every one of us must deal. It is certainly necessary to happiness, usefulness, and success. It is even necessary to survival. Many of us remember the words of Franklin Delano Roosevelt's 1945 Jefferson Day speech which he did not live to deliver: "Today we are faced with the pre-eminent fact that if civilization is to survive, we must cultivate the science of human relationships — the ability of all peoples, of all kinds, to live together and work together in the same world at peace."[1] Whether we agree with the word "science" or not, we certainly agree that we must learn to live together.

WE CAN LEARN

"Learn" is the word. We might say that for the first three

---

1 *New York Times,* April 14, 1945, p. 7, col. 1.

or more years of life a person can say, "I am what I am given." In the next few years, probably to about eleven or twelve, he is characterized by the words, "I am what I will." In the third period, adolescence, he says, "I am what I imagine I will be." Then, in the fourth period, which may extend to the grave, "I am what I learn."

The last of these is probably the most important and, in a way, goes back to childhood. Jesus expressed this idea in the words, "Unless you turn and become like children, you will never enter the kingdom of heaven" (Matt. 18:3 RSV). Children grow in their ability to get along with people. Unless we adults retrace our steps and unlearn some of our bad personal habits, open our minds to new patterns of conduct, there is no hope for us. That is what Jesus was saying, for one thing. Growth is not only "adding to" but also relearning. I have seen people sixty years of age "turn" and learn how to follow Jesus in dealing with people.

Lewis Mumford called man "the unfinished animal," and says, "Unlike other organisms, the final stage of growth is not determined by his biological past: it rests with himself and is partly determined by his own plans for the future."[2] Jesus said, "Come unto me and learn of me." It is precisely because we are not animals that this is possible.

Let us not suppose for a moment that getting along with people means being namby-pamby or just good natured, like the amiable alcoholic, Elwood, in the play *Harvey*. In one of his speeches Mary Chase has him say: "Dr. Chumley, my mother used to say to me, 'In this world, Elwood, you must be oh, so smart or oh, so pleasant.' For years I was smart. I recommend pleasant. You can quote me."[3]

Such relating to people is about as realistic and about as

---

2 Lewis Mumford, *The Conduct of Life* (New York: Harcourt Brace and Company, 1951), p. 36.
3 *Harvey* (New York: Dramatists Play Service, Inc., 1950), p. 49.

useful as that of another drunk who wandered into a saloon with a long list in his hand. When questioned about the list of names, he said, "Here, I have written all the names of the fellows in this town I can whip."

A burly chap asked, "Got my name on that list?"

"Yes, I have."

"Well, you can't whip me," said the man, drawing himself up to his full height.

"Okay," said the drunk, "I'll take your name off." Come to think of it, that was the result of some social learning!

One of the ways of improving our relations with our fellows is to look at some of the faulty techniques we use. The interesting thing about them, too, is that they all are dealt with in the New Testament. There never has been such a valuable book on human relations.

SCAPEGOATING

There is the bad technique of "scapegoating." This expression comes from the ancient Jewish practice of laying hands on a goat, confessing all the sins of the people over him, and then sending him away into the wilderness (see Lev. 16:20 ff.) on the Day of Atonement. It was as if he were the one who was at fault, the one who had sinned.

In modern times the term "scapegoating" has come to mean calling attention to the faults and evils of others in order to distract attention from our own. A scapegoat is anybody we blame for the trouble we are in. Hitler blamed the Jews for all of the deprivations he forced upon the people as he built up a war economy. As the Roman Empire crumbled, the Christians were blamed. In the Old Testament, Ahab said to Elijah, "Art thou he that troubleth Israel?" (See 1 Kings 18:17 ff.) When Paul came to Thessalonica the Jews shouted, "These that have turned the world upside down are come hither also" (Acts 17:6). It is hard for those who are failing to analyze honestly the reasons for failure and to change what is wrong. It is so much easier to blame someone else.

THE HALO TECHNIQUE

Closely associated with scapegoating is the "halo" technique. This is the practice of being perfect. One of my friends illustrated this perfectly in the words, "I am not the least bit conceited, but I don't know why I am not." Jesus pointed out this type in the person who says, "Let me help you get that speck out of your eye" while all the time there was a whole beam in the speaker's own eye. He dramatized the technique by telling of a man who stood and prayed, "God, I thank thee, that I am not as other men are . . . even as this publican." Pardon me while I adjust my halo! "Confess your faults one to another and pray for one another" (James 5:16).

THE THRONE TECHNIQUE

A third error in interpersonal relations, and one that is equally destructive to the self, is the "throne" technique. This is the method of individuals who regress to a childhood state of mind, or who never grow up. They need a master, a teacher, a leader, an adult to whom they can look and whom they honor. They have renounced their own God-given right of individuality and allowed someone else to stand on their feet. This is a form of projection, as the psychologists would say. It seems never to occur to such people that they are really in love with themselves — projected like a picture on a screen, onto an ideal person — and they live a life of fantasy imagining that they are like the person whom they worship.

The idol, or the person they have placed on a throne, may be a movie actor or actress, a millionaire, a college professor, a minister, or a gangster. The unfortunate thing about this type of a person is that his hero is just as likely to be inferior as not. Except in the case of those who worship Christ, the idol is bound to be inadequate. If something happens to shatter the image of such a hero worshiper, his own ego is shattered. That is why such people are so unrealistic; they have to be in order to hold on to their idol.

Jesus struck at the religious idols when He said, "Call no man your father upon the earth: for one is your Father, which is in heaven" (Matt. 23:9). He meant exactly what He said. For grown people to place one person on a throne and look up to him as one who can do no evil is disastrous to the growth of the soul. It is an easy life but a wrong one. In some social circles you see these characters and hear them gush, "Isn't he just divine?" Or, "He is the smartest man I have ever seen; he speaks seven languages." Admiration for those who are worthy is desirable, but it is easier to admire a great man than to become one. God calls us to become valuable people, not to worship them. And genuine people do not want to be put on a pedestal, much less on a throne.

LABELING

Another method which often destroys good human relations is the "labeling" technique. All of us hate to be called names. And some people seem never to realize that they can get just as bad results as a "cusser" without being profane. A man may not slap you for calling him narrow-minded, prudish, naïve, or old fogy, but he won't like you. The trouble with labels, you see, is that they are used to describe individuals as if that were all there is to the person. For example, "Smith is a neurotic." Is he neurotic all the time? And just wherein is he different from you or me? Smith may be honest, industrious, religious, and unselfish too.

Labels are devices used by talkative people to save them the trouble of thinking. Jesus warned against this hateful manner of speaking, "Whosoever shall say to his brother, . . . Thou fool, shall be in danger of hell fire" (Matt. 5:22).

IN THE DOGHOUSE

One of the most common ways of losing friends and hurting people is the "doghouse" technique. You make a mistake with some people, and they are off of you for life. The religious people in Jesus' day had tax collectors and sinners in the doghouse. Most of us can understand how they felt toward tax collectors, especially as we get nearer to April 15 each year. The sinners were not moral degenerates, but, according to the best Bible authorities, they were in general simply "nonpracticing Jews, ignorant or careless of the scribal laws." Jesus was known as "a friend of publicans and sinners."

It is common to find individuals who place whole classes of people in the doghouse. Sometimes the ones thus dealt with differ from them economically, sometimes racially, sometimes socially, sometimes religiously. But the person who has ostracized others in this way sees them as different kinds of human beings, and the more the difference is magnified the greater becomes the gulf between them. "The Jews have no dealings with the Samaritans."

I'LL-TAKE-MY-DOLLS-AND-GO-HOME

There is one other antisocial technique which all of us have practiced at one time or another; in childhood, if not since. It is the "I'll-take-my-dolls-and-go-home" technique. Our feelings are hurt, and we resign. We get a divorce. We quit the job. Even in church this pattern of conduct is sometimes seen. I have known people to drift from one church to another because in each new group they have had their feelings hurt and felt themselves deeply injured. We sometimes criticize them as "church tramps," but the facts are that it is easier to move on than it is to grow up.

Divorces are oftener than not the result of this "I'll-take-my-dolls-and-go-home" technique. A large percent of couples who separate could learn to live together if they did not resort to this revenge method. It is the easy — though childish — way. And as long as society adds its blessings to the "incompatibility" and "mental cruelty" types of divorce, people will be encouraged to remain immature.

PRINCIPLES OF GOOD HUMAN RELATIONS

Now let us look at the positive side of getting along with people. What are the principles of good human relations? How do we grow in this very important matter of living together? We Christians ought to be interested in this. Our religion stands for good relations, and none of us is perfect in this matter. "If it be possible, as much as lieth in you, live peaceably with all men" (Rom. 12:18).

But living together in good relations does not mean always living at peace with everyone. Jesus said: "I came not to send peace, but a sword. For I am come to set a man at variance against his father, . . ." (Matt. 10:34-36). We cannot always please man, if we are to obey God. Evil must be driven out, at times, just as Jesus drove the money changers out of the Temple. "Yes-men" and "me-too" Christians are not strong Christians. Jesus exposed the hypocrites of His day and rebuked them publicly. Paul withstood Peter to His face at Antioch "because he was to be blamed" (Gal. 2:11).

Most of our troubles arise from our not being unselfish and big enough to practice the principles of love and good will. We either will not use our imaginations enough to understand how the other fellow feels, or we do not love enough to relate ourselves to him. Some of us have learned in childhood to relate to people only on the basis of domination or cold justice (legalism), and we have not grown since. To some, we must be in the role of leadership; to some, we must be followers;

and, to most, we must relate as equals and sharers of responsibility. But in every case we are interdependent. We must interact. Isolation and segregation are dangerous. We need the love and acceptance of others as they need us. This requires flexibility and a constant strengthening of our ties with those about us.

COMMUNICATION

A primary principle in getting along with others is *communication*. When relations get bad between nations they "break off communication" and recall their ambassadors. It is just as true within family circles. I have known husbands and wives who would not speak to each other. At the breakfast table the father would say, "Jimmie, tell your mother to pass me the bacon." Sometimes we become so mad that we do not trust ourselves to talk. A man will say, "I would have gone to see the man and tried to talk it out with him, but I was afraid I would say something I would regret."

About the meanest sort of refusal to communicate is to refrain from the common courtesy of speaking to people. "I am through with that guy for life," a person says. Or as one man said to another, "I want you to promise me that you will never speak to me again as long as you live." The other replied calmly, "Well, I won't speak to you if I can remember it, but I may forget." One of the shrewdest statements the late George Bernard Shaw ever wrote was: "The worst sin towards our fellow creatures is not to hate them but to be indifferent to them. That's the essence of inhumanity."

Of course, talking is not always communicating. Some people talk to cover up their real anxieties, their real feelings. And the most polite people are often the most hostile. But by words, looks, smiles, gestures, we tell people how we feel about them. If we get too emotional with anger our words become "snarl" words. We show our lack of respect and block real communication.

Jesus placed communication as the basic means of good relations. "If thou bring thy gift to the altar, and there rememberest that thy brother hath aught against thee; leave there thy gift before the altar, and go thy way; first be reconciled to thy brother, and then come and offer thy gift" (Matt. 5:23-24). "If thy brother shall trespass against thee, go and tell him his fault between thee and him alone; if he shall hear thee, thou hast gained thy brother" (Matt. 18:15). The common factor in settling differences, whether one has offended or has been offended, is to talk it out. The Christian aim is to renew communications, whether the difficulty is in the church or between labor and capital, husband and wife, father and son, or business associates. I have known Ph.D.'s on university campuses who would not speak to each other. So regardless of education or social class, the principle is the same; communication is a prime essential in good human relations.

GROUP AUTHORITY

A second principle of good relations is *group authority*. Let the group decide.

This is precisely what Jesus said. In the passage in Matthew 18 we are instructed to talk first to the offender alone; then take one or two more; the third step is to "tell it to the church." The two last steps involve a very understandable fact, that individuals need the counsel of the group. A consensus as authority is inherent in the very meaning of democracy.

Let us look at an opposing viewpoint. Some would assert that the few are better equipped to instruct or to govern or to judge us than the many. Perhaps this is so. But I agree with C. S. Lewis that democracy is necessary because fallen men are "so wicked that not one of them can be trusted with any irresponsible power over his fellows." Authority must be exercised over small children, the mentally deficient, the insane, and criminals. But when fairly normal adults, however bright or saintly, claim to have authority over their fellows, real harm is done.

If the authority is accepted, immaturity on the part of both the dominated and the dominator results. If it is rejected by those being dominated, conflict arises. This is true in both politics and religion; and no amount of appeal to "divine right," the Scriptures, inspiration, or special revelation can justify one individual or minority group in dominating others.

The jury system in jurisprudence rests upon this need for a consensus. Congregational government in churches is the same. In politics it is the representative form of government. In intellectual matters the technique of discussion is based upon this principle. Of course, the majority opinion will not always represent the truth — perhaps seldom, in some fields — but it must be recognized if people are to get along together.

"I want your advice" or "I should like to discuss a matter with you" are words of humility. We need to check our opinions on morals, religion, politics, and any other subject by discussing them with our fellows. As we come alive in Christ, we will know that only the group which has a similar experience will be able to counsel us on matters pertaining to the kingdom of God. In some situations only God can guide us in the true way. Sometimes, to be in such a situation seems precarious. That is, ideas of such divine guidance sometimes seem close to certain insane delusions to non-believers. "We ought to obey God rather than men" is a true Christian attitude, but the men who said that were closely knit into a Christian group.

PERMISSIVENESS

A third principle of good human relations is *permissiveness*. This is the opposite of domination and criticism. It applies to normal relations between adults. Actually, it applies to nearly all affairs where one human being comes into contact with another. The permissive attitude says: "I accept you as the unique person you are. You may chart your own course, make your own mistakes, say what you really feel, and you will not be frowned at or criticized unless you attempt to hurt or destroy someone."

Permissiveness requires that advice be given, if at all, only in a circumstance where it may be rejected without punishment. Suggestions are proposed with perfect freedom for them to be rejected. All attempts at coercion are carefully avoided. In this setting, teaching and preaching become the imparting of knowledge, the testimony of personal experiences, or the description of reality and the invitation to or offer of a particular advantage or blessing.

Nothing but faith in individuals and in God can undergird this attitude. It expresses great respect for people and great faith in their ability to make valuable decisions.

Jesus gives us many examples in the way He dealt with people. The rich young ruler "went away sorrowful" when the demands of discipleship were made plain; most of us would have followed him and brought pressure to bear on him. Peter was warned but not browbeaten concerning his denial. The Pharisees were exposed and told of their destiny because they were destroying life. But Jesus was so permissive toward tax-collectors and sinners that they "drew near to hear him" — and the religious leaders murmured, saying, "This man receiveth sinners, and eateth with them." He also dined in the home of Simon the Pharisee and welcomed an interview with Nicodemus. And did any leader ever show as much patience and acceptance as He did toward Peter and other erring disciples? Jesus' method was exactly the opposite of the "doghouse" technique.

TRICKS OF DOMINATION

Attempts to dominate have left a long trail of blood and human misery across the centuries. Besides the Spanish Inquisition there have been many little private "trials of heretics" in homes, churches, and schools. We have used pressure methods all the way from ridicule to promise of eternal bliss. Most of these methods have not been due to our conceit and immodesty but to a more vicious motive of will to power or desire for omnipotence.

Tricks of dominance are often subtle and appear as very noble virtues. *Shame* is one of these. "Aren't you ashamed of yourself for even thinking such a thing?" a parent may say. Then the real feelings are driven underground, and the ugly emotion continues to operate. *Pity* is another. "Look how much I have done for you; surely you are going to do what I ask you" may be merely a method of enforcing demands. *Fear* is an equally effective one. "God will punish you if you neglect your duty" has been used to whip people in line. *Offer of approval* also is used to coerce. "People will not like you unless you learn to co-operate." All of these and many more are used daily by human beings, but they do not produce growth. Jesus never used these on His disciples. He appealed to love and voluntary loyalty. Threat of hell or hope of heaven were used more as the description of reality than as incentives or means of control.

For example, the words "Ye will not come to me, that ye might have life" are sad words — William Lyon Phelps once said that they are the saddest words in the English language — but they leave the individual free. "What does it profit a man if he gains the whole world and loses his own soul?" is a searching, disturbing question, but its force is in the reality principle back of it. All of us must feel the pressure of reality.

FORGIVENESS

The last principle in getting along with people is *forgiveness*. This handles situations where injuries, real or seeming, have occurred. And occur they will. When you meet a person who is hard to hurt, you see one who does not love deeply. It is no compliment to be able to say, "No one can insult me; I just don't pay any attention to them." The finest people in this world are sensitive people who are hurt deeply when they are misunderstood, who really want to love and to be loved.

Under the spell of some evangelistic services a very fine woman in a small town began to worry about her neighbor. They had "fallen out" over a milk bill. There were no ugly words. Both were courteous but cool. As they had gone along, each had secretly harbored a grudge against the other. The revival had caused some self-examination.

The first woman finally got up nerve to go to the second and say, "I feel awful about that misunderstanding we had last year, etc." The second was a Christian also. She accepted the apology of the first woman and then admitted that she had been wrong. She sought forgiveness, too. There was a joy in their hearts which they had been deprived of for many months.

We remember that Jesus said that we must be willing to forgive an unlimited number of times (Matt. 18:21-22). Furthermore, He said that we can be forgiven our sins only as we forgive others (Matt. 6:14-15). If this is true, some people whom I know have been wasting their time praying for forgiveness of their sins. They may have withheld punishment from those who have hurt them, but that is not forgiveness.

WHAT FORGIVENESS MEANS

Forgiveness involves three things. First of all, the person who has been injured accepts the injury. He bears a cross. In order to do this, he must be mature enough to be honest about his injury and mature enough to accept suffering. In the second place, forgiveness means helping the sufferer bear the burden of his sin. Joseph said to his brothers who had sold him into slavery, "Be not grieved or angry with yourselves." When a person really forgives, he gets under the load of the offender, and their former fellowship and understanding is restored.

All of these examples are illustrated in the Cross. In accepting forgiveness through the Cross we come to see that God accepts the injury of our sin, relieves us of our feeling of guilt, and brings us into a close relationship with Himself. The same process occurs in human forgiveness. Fellowship is rebuilt. Each person involved actively shows good will toward the other.

People being what they are, forgiveness is a very important part of getting along with one another. Those who never seek or offer forgiveness either relate to others on a very superficial basis or never obey God in rebuilding broken or disturbed relationships. Some husbands and wives drift apart and never get close again because they do not forgive. And we are such sinners that church members must again and again ask one another to forgive. Only in this way can the full power of God be fully experienced in human life.

A control operator in a radio station had a misunderstanding with another operator. Some deep feelings were involved. The first operator heard a sermon on the Matthew 18 passage about how to straighten out difficulties; the preacher insisted that it would work. He tried it, and to his pleasure he and the other operator became good friends. It was the first operator's initial step to Christ. He had felt himself a failure in getting along with people. Now he had found a real help. "I thought to myself," he said, "If Jesus Christ knew what he was talking about in that matter, I would try Him in others also. That's how I came to be a Christian."

CHAPTER FOURTEEN

Consider The Lilies How They Grow

"Consider the lilies of the field, how they grow" were just words to me for years. Of course, they were beautiful. Fields of beautiful flowers waving in the breeze, wilting in the hot sun; standing dew-laden, fresh and crisp in the early morning; these images make us warm with delight. But the relation between lilies and everyday life was not clear.

It was not too difficult to "spiritualize" such a passage and draw analogies between the growth of a lily and human existence. Matthew Henry talked about the fact that a lily is "frail"; it is "free from care"; it is "fair and fine." These similarities do not impress me. Of course we are frail — so what? We do not have to live long before we learn that human beings cannot remain "free from care." It does not seem to be even intended for us. And few of us are fine or fair. We are deformed, ugly, deficient, inadequate — at least, some of us are. Jesus must have meant something by these words which would apply to all of us at all times, to both the fine and the disfigured.

Then, one day, I noticed that I was saying to individuals who came to me for counsel, "Consider the lilies how they grow." At first, they looked puzzled. Then, there was a look of I'm-beginning-to-catch-on.

Here is a case in point. At a given place in a series of interviews, a man said to me, "I see now what caused me to have

177

this trouble, and I want to overcome it. What do I do next?"
I could outline a way of life for him or tell him a lot about
how to "think positively" about his circumstances. Not only
would such suggestions do no permanent good, but they would
actually do harm. To act as a father to another human being
usually prolongs his state of immaturity. And there are no
trick mental methods to produce growth. So I said, "Consider
the lilies how they grow."

An explanation was in order. For one thing, I told him
that he was trying too hard. Such attempts at growth do not
produce the desired result; they block it. He was very emotional. "What do I do next?" meant to him that he must do
something in a hurry. He was prepared to put forth a great
effort. My feeling was that "easy does it."

WHAT JESUS MEANT

Let us look now at what Jesus really meant by this remark.
It is in that passage in the Sermon on the Mount which deals
with worry. Many people who read books on how to stop
worrying would do well to save their money and read Matthew 6:25-34. It is the divine recipe for handling normal
worry. I say normal because many people who are emotionally
sick need psychotherapy, just as cancer patients need X-ray
treatments.

Jesus gave His disciples six distinctive approaches to the
problem of worry: (1) Life, or the real person, is more important than the "things" we are worrying about; we must value
our true selves. (2) It does no good to worry — which of you
by worrying can add one cubit to your stature? (3) You must
learn to trust God your Heavenly Father, "O ye of little faith."
(4) First things must be put first — "Seek ye first the kingdom
of God." (5) Each day has its own troubles, and only its
own (v. 34) — so, live one day at a time. (6) He has divinely

ordained means of growth and daily provision for us, just as He does for the birds and the flowers.

It is the expression, "Consider the lilies how they grow," or as Williams says, "Look at the wild lilies and learn how they grow," that especially interests me. Why did He not say, "See how they stand"? Or, "See how they surpass other flowers in beauty"! Instead He said, "How they grow." This may mean nothing more than, "See how they normally become the admired flower." In any case, He took the flower as an illustration of the kind of individuals we may become.

It is of little consequence to us that the word translated lily probably referred to the red anemone which dots all of the hillsides of Galilee in the spring. Actually, no species of the lily is a conspicuous feature of the flora of Palestine. This word may merely refer to "wild flowers" and is so used often, the scholars tell us. Jesus' use of it is merely that. He takes the beautiful flower and says, in effect: "Look at how it grows naturally. All of the robes of Solomon were not as beautiful." How does the lily get that way? By struggling? By effort? By trying hard? "No," He says, "it simply expressed the life within it and became what God created it to be."

Then Jesus draws a further analogy. If these plants, beautiful as they are, lasting only for a brief season, are so well taken care of, what about you, O you who have such little faith? These are striking words. He has a real point; perhaps several. But most of the world seems to have read right over them.

If I wished to spiritualize this famous quotation I could draw many analogies to the tender, beautiful plant. Growth for the flower and for us is very slow. We must depend on external nourishment, especially sunlight. We must suffer an environment which is often adverse and hostile. Sooner or later we will be cut down. But these are not the lessons Jesus had in mind. Tennyson was nearer the spirit of this passage in his little "Flower in the Crannied Wall" lines:

> Flower in the crannied wall,
> I pluck you out of the crannies,
> I hold you here, root and all, in my hand,
> Little flower — but *if* I could understand
> What you are, root and all, and all in all,
> I should know what God and man is.

Both Tennyson and Jesus felt that the life of the flower and the life of the human spirit are closely related to the Living God.

The Christian, like the lily, grows naturally, unfolding the life that is within. The Christian, mind you, not the unsaved person. "He who has the Son has life; he who has not the Son has not life" (1 John 5:12 RSV). The Sermon on the Mount, in which Jesus suggested that the lilies be considered, was spoken to disciples, to believers. It is natural for a Christian to grow as it is for the heart of a living person to beat. In this day of "activism" such an outlook on life must appear dead wrong. But it is not.

Did you ever see a person really grow by *trying?* "We can do nearly anything if we try hard enough," we have all heard. I will go so far as to say that clinching your fist, putting out your chin, and tensing your body for a struggle will not help you to grow but will definitely hinder your growth. Every Christian who is a careful observer, of himself and others, knows this to be so.

The first requirement of growth then is in being somebody to start with. Becoming is preceded by being. By this we do not mean simply the popular idea of self-acceptance. Rather, we must form a concept of ourselves as the unique persons which God made us to be. We must become individuals. The "I" must be the true "I", not the sham self or the mask or the idol which we imagine ourselves to be. This is what modern psychologists call "ego-identity." It is self-consciousness in the best sense of the word. It is the way the "I" thinks of the "me."

YOUR PICTURE OF YOURSELF

What kind of a picture do you have of yourself? Perhaps we have different pictures hanging on different walls in our lives. Some of them may be caricatures. Are you smart, ugly, kind, conceited, cowardly, sissy, weak, flexible, or a dozen other adjectives which might be used? Unfortunately, many people think of themselves solely in terms of the "tags" which society places on them, determined usually in terms of their "market value." From kindergarten to college, we try to educate a person to become "marketable." Our only concern seems to be in producing people who can make "big money," be the top man on the totem pole, be the best of something or other. A few hours before a TV set will prove that. We are alienated from our true selves, so we have to try to live up to the false selves which we have created. Harriet Beecher Stowe records that she went to a party where "everyone seems to have left themselves at home."

If self-acceptance means settling down to live with this "sham self," I do not want any part of it. The prodigal son was pursuing the sham self when he demanded his property so that he could "have a good time." But later he came to himself (Luke 15:17). He then started to grow from the core of the personality God had given him. He could not deal with the "ought" until he came to grips with the "is" of human existence. The painful reality of the real self must be faced before growth can take place.

Imagine a lily trying to be a violet. Or for that matter, imagine one kind of lily trying to be one of another species. That is no more absurd than for one human being to try to be like another. "Solomon in all of his glory" was not supposed to be superior to a lily. It is this everlasting rejection of God's creativity which brings us worry and waste. To wish that we

were like someone else, or superior to him, is downright insolence to God. The beginning of all spiritual growth is the will
to be unique.

Christian growth, then, consists not only in a man's coming
to himself but in a constant revision of our self-concepts. It is
the divinely ordained means of growth. If we allow anyone to
prescribe for us the kind of self which we are to be or if we
refuse to think about our true selves, there is no hope for us.
To grow we must stay conscious. Some people think that we
grow toward our ideals, but this is too intellectual. Actually,
we grow toward the picture of the selves we are in love with.
This loved image may be secret and unconscious. It may have
come from a parent, a movie, a book, a neighbor, or even be a
creation of our own; but, once we are in love with it, the control over our lives is automatic. Therefore, we must constantly
revise it in line with the self which God created.

Nowhere does the rejection of the real self become more
noticeable than in the treatment of children. A noted psychiatrist, Dr. Robert W. White, of Harvard University says:

> Rearing and guiding children can best be represented by the
> metaphor of raising plants. This should be encouraging, be-
> cause raising plants is one of mankind's most successful ac-
> tivities. Perhaps the success comes from the fact that the hus-
> bandman does not try to thrust impossible patterns on his
> plants. He respects their peculiarities, tries to provide suitable
> conditions, protects them from the more serious kinds of in-
> jury — but he lets the plants do the growing. He does not
> poke at the seed in order to make it sprout more quickly, nor
> does he seize the shoot when it breaks the ground and try to
> pull open the first leaves by hand. Neither does he trim the
> leaves of different plants in order to have them all look alike.
> It is the children who must do the growing, and they can do
> it only through the push of their own budding interests![1]

Another aspect of considering the lilies, which Jesus may

---

1 Robert W. White, *Lives in Progress* (New York: Dryden Press, 1952), p.
363.

have had in mind and closely related to the meaning of the whole passage, is this: a lily must grow where its bulb is planted. Or in the case of many flowers, where the seed is sown. The environment is not always favorable. Jesus in this passage on worry referred to the birds in this manner, "Yet your heavenly Father feedeth them." In other words, all of God's creation, even plants that spring up for a season and then perish, are under His "providing eye" — we call it providence.

Most of the attempts to prove providence leave me cold and unconvinced. I do not believe that we can prove chance, mechanism, or providence. To me pantheism, with everything being god, and deism, with its far-off god, seem to me to be a blinder faith than a belief in a God who looks after the sparrow and numbers the hairs on our heads. Philosophy cannot answer the question of happenings. Faith must step in and show us that the God who revealed himself in Christ causes all things to "work together for good to them that love God" (Rom. 8:28). This is a faith.

SPIRITUAL FIXATION

For this discussion, the important point is that growth depends on our taking the right attitude toward our environment, physical or human. If we do not, growth stops. The psychologists speak of this as "fixation." A person has a very painful experience, one that produces anxiety, and growth (at least in an area) stops. A lily can stand just so much cold weather, for example; and a human being can stand just so much anxiety, insecurity, and frustration. Every person has his "tension capacity." Beyond that capacity, he will develop protective symptoms, become stereotyped, withdraw, become belligerent, or perhaps go insane. These extreme reactions are much more complex than I have indicated, but they are reactions to stress and strain.

All of us have seen people who were "spiritually fixated." "My mother made me go to Sunday school when I was a boy, so I made up my mind that if I ever got big enough I would stop." This is easy to see when a person talks about it, but it is equally operative in those who are not that honest. Sometimes a disagreement with a friend, loss of a job, a death, an illness, a handicap, a few nights of insomnia, or even confusion over an intellection problem, may stop us from growing.

Somerset Maugham, in *The Summing Up,* gives us an illustration of how a very threatening situation caused him to lose faith in God:

> I had not been long in school before I discovered, through the ridicule to which I was exposed and the humiliations I suffered, how great a misfortune it was to me that I stammered; and I had read in the Bible that if you had faith you could move mountains. My uncle assured me that it was a literal fact. One night, when I was going back to school next day, I prayed to God with all my might that He would take away my impediment; and, such was my faith, I went to sleep quite certain that when I awoke next morning I should be able to speak like everybody else. I pictured to myself the surprise of the boys (I was still at preparatory school) when they found I no longer stammered. I woke full of exultation and it was a real, a terrible shock, when I discovered that I stammered as badly as ever.[2]

I have seen people stop growing, sometimes for a short time, at various ages. The most critical periods seem to be adolescence, middle age (from forty to fifty-five particularly), and later maturity (beyond retirement age). The environment becomes difficult, the individual loses hope, and soon he turns within himself.

The way we look upon events has a lot to do with continued growth. Did you ever turn over a thin rock, lying lightly

---

2 Somerset Maugham, *The Summing Up* (New York: Alfred A. Knopf, Inc., 1938), pp. 153, 154.

on the top of the ground, and see there a plant which the sunlight had never touched? The seed sprouted and the tender
shoots pushed hard against the severe stone, to no avail. Then
the shoot just grew around, crooked and pale, and that is the
way winter found it. Some lives are like that. They are underprivileged lives, we often think. But are they?

My faith tells me that there are no underprivileged lives
except those which reject the privileges which are offered.
Each life has grace for its grind and comfort for its circum-
scriptions. Some insecurity and blockings are undoubtedly
ordained of God to make us walk by faith. When the outlook
gets bad, we often are forced to an upward look. Unhappiness, tension, frustration, crosses, are a part of the Christian
life just as the blasting heat, the twisting wind, and the footsteps of animals are a part of the lily's environment. We must
grow where God plants us.

GETTING OFF BALANCE

Finally, real growth takes place, in the lily or in the human
being, as a process of getting off balance and on again. This
may seem a little odd at first. But growth is possible because
there is in all living things some kind of automatic self-regula-
tor which keeps the organism functioning. The scientists speak
of it as "homeostasis." When we eat too much food, it is
stored in the body; when we eat too little, the storehouse is
raided. When germs attack, the whole system is mobilized to
throw them off. A biologist writes: "Every organism is so built,
whether by mechanical principles or not, that every deviation
from the equilibrium point sets up a tendency to return to it."

The biologists and botanists know that all living things are
in a constant state of adjustment. For impersonal living organisms this adjustment is regulated by such growth factors as
catalysts, hormones, light, temperature, and many others. But
in human beings this matter of balance is, in addition to its be-

ing influenced by the physical, largely a matter of consciousness. Just as our bodies get hungry, tired, "keyed up" (or tense), and then come back to normal, so our souls get out of kelter and have to be brought back to equilibrium.

Many Christians seem to feel that they should never experience any anxiety or tension or temptation. And some almost achieve that state, but they are not growing Christians. Elton Trueblood is correct when he says:

> It is not the poise of perfect balance that moves mankind forward on his zigzag path, but the glorious immoderation of those who see something so clearly that they are willing to live and die for it. Such abandon seems tumultuous, but it actually produces a species of inner peace, for it helps to overcome crippling anxiety. The only way in which a man can move forward in what we call walking is by always being slightly out of balance, since the perfectly balanced man stands still. History moves forward as the balance is recurrently broken and restored.[3]

Life moves along a zigzag course. Our moods even swing like a pendulum. "Sometimes I'm up, sometimes I'm down, O yes Lord," says the Negro spiritual. Like Simon Peter walking on the water we cry, "Lord save me, or I perish." We feel as if we are going to pieces. Actually, the mind and soul of man are both very tough.

Of course, real character consists of a "steady" state. The great Christian may have turmoil within, like milk beating about in a churn. He may have inner conflict and psychic (soul) pain, but that does not prove that he is a weakling. The strong soul puts one foot in front of another and does the will of God until it becomes easier to do it. Or he says, "No" to temptation even when it is most alluring. This is the end of

---

3 Elton Trueblood, *The Life We Prize* (New York: Harper and Row, Publishers, 1951), p. 163.

the Christian life, and to be perfectly frank, is never fully attained in this world.

In the meantime, growth consists of trial and error, effort and failure, but also attempt and attainment. In home life we all see illustrations of these unbalanced states. The tender-minded become disturbed and seek a divorce. The tough-minded realize that the person who is "off center" needs two things; someone to associate with him who is strong and patient and loving, against whom he may bounce; and second, time. God gives us both. "Like as a father pitieth his children, so the Lord pitieth them that fear him. For he knoweth our frame; he remembereth that we are dust" (Psalm 103:13-14).

Perhaps some of us would like to claim that we never get off balance; our opinions are never colored by our prejudices, and our decisions are never entirely bad. A few people may convince themselves of that, but most of us know better. The best of us get off balance at times. In fact, growth depends on imbalances. We may even go further and say, as Trueblood hinted, that the will to grow is so strong in a living Christian that if he is balanced he will deliberately find a way to be unbalanced.

I have seen this over and over in churches. If a church does not have a creative program which requires adjustment, the real Christians will be very frustrated because they feel the need of growth and challenges. But those church members who are not growing, while the monotony will bore them some, have learned to insulate themselves by maintaining a kind of "peace of mind." To the living, monotony may be as disturbing as change. The dead are perfectly balanced.

Maintaining Equilibrium

By now, it is obvious that what we are aiming at in Christianity is not returning to any former state of equilibrium but the "steady state" of successful change and the speedy change to the right track when we find ourselves astray. "Let any one who thinks that he stands take heed lest he fall" (1 Cor. 10: 12 RSV). Counselors often find themselves saying to individuals, "You will just have to walk a tight rope for a while." What Jesus was trying to get across in the passage in Matthew was this: you may be walking a tight rope — in fact, you always are, from a human standpoint — but there is a mysterious aid that is always present. We are never alone, and hands greater than our own are holding us.

It is our faith that makes us veer back into the narrow path when we have gone astray. We never retrace our steps or take up where we have left off. What we do is to regain our spiritual balance.

The old-fashioned Bible terms for this process are as new and up-to-date in meaning, when properly understood, as the morning newspaper.

We must confess our sins, the Bible says. At a given point in therapy the psychiatrist or counselor must lead the individual to give up old "defense mechanisms." What is the difference? Perhaps there is more of the unconscious in the latter; but, sooner or later, the individual must say, "I have failed."

Then there is repentance. It is a "change of mind," the theologians say. But they also see more than that in it. The Bible speaks of it as "repentance toward God." Growth in human beings involves growth in interpersonal relations. The blocking in this sphere is, primarily, wrong attitudes. When we repent we renounce our independence, shed our insulations (that shut us from God), and acknowledge our status as subjects of God and fellow workers with men. Every sin is a denial of God's rights and an assertion of our own. Therefore, repentance is a part of growth, the divinely ordained means of maintaining spiritual balance.

Faith is also a part of the growth process. Trust is perhaps a better word, and its opposite is mistrust. Erik Erikson applies it to young children by saying that trust "implies not only that one has learned to rely on the sameness and continuity of the outer providers, but also that one may trust oneself and the capacity of one's own organs to cope with urges; and that one is able to consider oneself trustworthy enough so that the providers will not need to be on guard lest they be nipped." Erikson makes the point that "basic mistrust" of others goes back to infancy and that growth consists of learning that sense of belonging which means security. Without it we do not grow.

Jesus was trying to inspire that basic trust for growth. "Now if God so gorgeously dresses the wild grass which today is green and tomorrow is tossed into the furnace, will He not much more surely clothe you, O you with little faith?" (v. 30 Williams).

> Lord of all growing things,
> By such sweet, secret influences as those
> That draw the scilla through the melting snows,
> And bid the fledgling bird trust untried wings,
> When quick my spirit grows,
> Help me to trust my wings.
>
> AUTHOR UNKNOWN